90

D0613173

IN THE PIRATE'S DEN

MY LIFE AS A SECRET AGENT FOR CASTRO

JORGE MASETTI

ENCOUNTER BOOKS
SAN FRANCISCO

First edition published in 2002 by Encounter Books, an activity of Encounter for Culture and Education, Inc., a nonprofit tax exempt corporation.

Originally published in France as *La Loi des Corsaires, itinéraire d'un enfant de la révolution cubaine* in 1993 by Editions Stock.

Encounter Books website address: www.encounterbooks.com

Manufactured in the United States and printed on acid-free paper.

The paper used in this publication meets the minimum requirements of ANSI/NISO Z39.48-1992 (R 1997) (*Permanence of Paper*).

Library of Congress Cataloging-in-Publication Data

Masetti, Jorge, 1955–
   [Loi des corsaires. English]
   In the pirate's den : my life as a secret agent for Castro / Jorge Masetti.
      p.   cm.
      Includes index.
      ISBN 1-893554-42-2 (alk. paper)
      1. Masetti, Jorge, 1955– 2. Spies—Cuba—Biography.
   3. Espionage, Cuban—History—20th century.   I. Title.
   UB271.C92 M37513 2002
   327.127291\rquote 0092—dc21
   [B]

                                                    2002067518

                        10   9   8   7   6   5   4   3   2   1

Contents

Prologue
HAVANA, JUNE 1989

BOUT A MONTH BEFORE THE EVENTS I'm about to describe, I returned from Angola, where I had stayed for four months. It had not been like my usual visits. Previously I had always gone alone, secretly, under a false identity, as befits someone involved in "special operations." But this time I had traveled legally, representing a legitimate commercial enterprise and accompanied by my wife, Ileana.

As soon as I returned to Havana, I went to meet with Colonel Antonio de la Guardia—"Tony" to his friends—who was my boss, as well as my father-in-law and a friend. He looked the same as always: short and stocky with a shining bald head and handsome face. To those of us involved in Cuban intelligence operations, he was a legendary figure. He was the commander of Cuba's Special Troops—Fidel's equivalent of America's elite Delta Force or the CIA's paramilitaries. During the euphoric days when we convinced ourselves that a hemispheric revolution was possible, he had organized a personal bodyguard of Cubans for Salvador Allende, and he was there when Allende was overthrown and committed suicide. He also had fought alongside the Sandinistas in Nicaragua. Now he was in charge of an operation simply called MC (for *moneda convertible,* or convertible currency), the crucially important effort of Cuban intelligence to earn foreign exchange for the failing Cuban economy.

As always, Tony greeted me with a smile—the same smile that could look unyielding to those who had run up against him when he was raising funds for the Revolution. Tony was always cheerful, even in the most difficult times; but on this day, he seemed happier than usual. We sat on his patio under a beautiful climbing plant, the place

1

we always met when we had delicate matters to discuss. To reach the patio, you first passed through the terrace where Tony hung the brilliantly colored canvasses he had painted as a respite from his years amid the labyrinth of politics and espionage.

"Now we won't have to play at being businessmen anymore," he said, alluding to the work I had been doing in Africa under his direction. "Fortunately I have been relieved of commercial functions and can concentrate on special assignments. You will come to work with me in that section." Tony knew that I didn't like commercial jobs either. He was glad that Fidel Castro had abandoned his plan to employ the international experience of our professional revolutionary cadres in entrepreneurial activities, which had been designed to prop up the Revolution in its moment of economic crisis.

Now we could resume our real work, the "black" work of espionage and covert undertakings. I had repeatedly asked Tony to return me to such missions. At last, it seemed, we were ready to go.

"Rest up for a few days and get your documentation ready, because soon you'll have to leave for Spain and set up a base of operations there. I'll give you more details later," he added briefly, discouraging any further questions.

I was intrigued and would have liked to find out more about my special missions but I dared not ask anything further. I was accustomed to getting instructions instead of explanations regarding our type of work.

Our conversation then turned to family matters, when Ileana and Tony's wife, Mari, joined us. Tony seemed particularly affectionate toward Ileana. He hadn't seen her for months. She had accompanied me to Angola, not as the daughter of Tony de la Guardia, but simply as the wife of one of his officers, without the special privileges that might have been accorded to a relative of someone who was part of the Cuban power elite. Ileana had traveled with me even though Tony at first seemed to have reservations about the trip and especially about her going along.

"Mari, break open a bottle so we can toast both the return and the marriage of these two," he said with his customary joviality.

When Ileana and I married a few days before leaving for Angola, Tony could not attend because he was away on business. Now he seemed happy, proud of his daughter and of me too. He hugged and kissed her with great affection, as if trying to make up for his absences when she was a girl because of his constant secret missions abroad— so secret that he wasn't even allowed to write home. Now he could dote on her and give her what he wasn't able to before, and—although he didn't know it yet—what he would never be able to give her again.

After that emotional reunion, we went to the home of Tony's identical twin brother, Patricio—General Patricio de la Guardia. Ileana and I had been in touch with him more than with Tony lately. He had headed the Cuban Ministry of the Interior's mission in Angola for the last three years, and had returned to Havana just a few days earlier.

"Did you talk with Tony already, Terrorist?" Patricio always called me this. "You should be very happy. You will be able to do what you enjoy." He slapped me on the shoulder, evidently aware of what I would be doing, though not yet telling me anything about it.

The conversation with him was less formal than with Tony. Patricio was not my direct boss, and not my father-in-law. He had always treated me like one of his own, someone he could talk to, reveal his uncertainties to, and stop playing the general to for a while. I asked him what the new mission would be. He responded with a loud outburst of laughter.

"Now they've really gone crazy," he said, referring to Fidel's spymasters. "Working under Tony, you're going to set up a base of operations in Spain, and use it to launch operations in the United States. Believe it or not, the first objective is to blow up the transmission balloon of TV Martí!"

I froze. It was one thing to operate in Latin America, where I had worked for years, or even in Europe or Africa, and quite another to work in the United States, especially in efforts against TV Martí, a multimillion-dollar project, begun by the Reagan administration a few years earlier, to beam a powerful television signal into Cuba carrying information and propaganda against the Revolution and against Fidel Castro personally. I imagined the layers of protection such an enterprise must have. Nevertheless, I knew that if this was Tony's job, he'd get it done. He had built a career out of fulfilling missions even more ambitious than this one, and had always come back victorious. He was, without a doubt, the most qualified man in Cuba to direct this kind of operation.

I relaxed. If they had chosen me it was because Tony had confidence in me, Patricio had confidence in me, and the Revolution had confidence in me. It meant I had earned the right to be a full participant in such a delicate mission. After our talk, Patricio and I agreed to meet for dinner with our wives later on.

Patricio came to pick us up at eight. He brought along a bag that I had loaned him when he last left for Angola; inside it was the $10,000 that Tony had instructed him to give me as the first installment of the money I would need to set up shop in Spain. After stashing it away, we went to a restaurant, and then Ileana and I decided to spend the night at the home of Tony and Patricio's parents, who were at the center of this large patriarchal family.

Returning home the next morning, we noticed that our apartment had been searched. Nothing was gone, but the intruders had obviously taken great care to leave everything exactly as it had been. But they missed one thing: a small, wadded-up piece of paper that I had left near the door, as I had done habitually for years. The little ball had been moved, revealing that someone had entered in our absence.

I immediately went to Patricio and told him about this. He answered with a laugh: "Come on, Terrorist, don't forget you're in Cuba. Who is going to search you here? You're not in Argentina or Colombia. This is our country, our fortress. Don't be paranoid."

This sounded reasonable. Nevertheless, I was certain that someone had illicitly entered and it wasn't thieves, because nothing was missing—not my guns, not my money. I had a queasy feeling.

That afternoon, still shaken, I went with Ileana to her great-aunt's place at the beach. I wasn't the only one who felt things weren't quite right. Ileana spent our last night at the beach crying. She said she suspected that something horrible was about to happen. Since I have always let myself be guided by my own presentiments and those of others, I began to fret, thinking that the operation in the United States would go wrong, or that maybe the Americans would find out what we were up to and perhaps kill one of us in Cuba.

During the next three days, at various times and in different places, I thought I saw the same white car with the same faces inside; but I told myself that Patricio was probably right and the many years of rigorous clandestine protocols had ended up making me somewhat paranoid. What was I worried about? I was in Cuba, after all.

We returned to Havana for Tony and Patricio's birthday party. Everyone was looking forward to the event. Because they were so rarely at home, it had been years since the twins had together celebrated the occasion with the family. Who knew when they would have another chance?

We were expected to be there punctually at lunch time, but since it was June 13 and I'm superstitious, I drove very slowly, so we were an hour late. When we pulled up at the grandparents' house, the whole family was there except for Tony and Patricio. Grandmother Mimi was furious. "How is it possible," she demanded, "that after so many years of separation, these boys leave me with lunch on the table on their own birthday?"

Ileana's 89-year-old grandfather, Popín, was more patient. He told Mimi to wait, for surely the twins had been delayed by some urgent responsibility. But as the afternoon progressed and neither had arrived, everyone agreed that something was wrong. Grandmother's bad mood worsened, and I also grew worried. It was June 13, 1989. Tuesday the thirteenth, an unlucky day ...

Finally, Ileana and I decided to go to Patricio's house, which was closest, to see what was up. We rang the bell several times. Strangely, all the windows were closed, which prevented us from looking inside. After a while, a tall, light-skinned black man opened the door. He was dressed in civilian clothes, but had the unmistakable look of a policeman. I immediately understood that the situation was grave, and I solemnly asked for "the General," not "Patri" as I usually called him. Instead of answering, he asked us who we were. I didn't know how to answer.

And then we heard the voice of Patricio's wife, Isabel, a young woman with olive skin and chestnut hair who held a plum job selling goods to tourists for hard currency. "Let them in," she said, coming to greet us. "It's Tony's daughter and her husband." Weeping, she told us, "Tony and Patricio are prisoners in Villa Marista."

Villa Marista was a name to cause shivers. Formerly a Marist monastery, it had been taken over during the Revolution and made into the headquarters of the Cuban political police, where they imprisoned dissidents.

"I don't know what's happening," Isabel kept saying, her face sagging in despair. "I just don't know what is happening."

I will never forget the interior of the house. Possessions were scattered all over the floor. Five or six men were systematically searching, dismantling, prying into every corner of the house. I was stunned to see revolutionary symbols being thrown about indiscriminately along with various trivia. There, strewn on the floor and trampled, were the olive-drab and camouflage uniforms Patricio had worn on so many campaigns, his general's stars and the medals he had won on international missions, the handguns, even the enormous portrait of Che Guevara beneath which Ileana and I had been photographed on the day of our wedding to seal our commitment to fighting for the Revolution.

I felt as though I were chewing on broken glass. Amidst the litter on the floor I imagined I could see the body of my father and those of my companions who also had fallen in the struggle for the Revolution: Santiago, Pedro Pacho, Belomo....

Without thinking, I stammered: "This is incredible!"

But the cold voice of the man who had opened the door brought me back to reality: "Why 'incredible'? Don't you have faith in the Revolution?"

1

HAVANA, MAY 1965

WHEN WAS MY REVOLUTIONARY FAITH—the faith that would begin to die in Patricio de la Guardia's house that afternoon first born? I think it was on one of those hot and humid May afternoons in Havana in 1965, when the evocative perfume of the mango blossom suffuses everything.

Possibly I was running after a ball. Or chasing a frightened lizard. Maybe I was trying to catch a butterfly. I'm not sure; I was only ten years old.

Absorbed in my games and inebriated by the aroma of the afternoon, I didn't notice right away that Comandante Piñeiro was beckoning me from the doorway of his house. His full name was Manuel Piñeiro Losada, and he had been with Fidel and particularly his brother Raúl since their first push out of the mountains in 1958. Already familiar to me, he would became a fact of my life for the next twenty-five years. He was an imposing man, although he had the affable demeanor of one of those Santa Clauses who visit American shopping centers during Christmas—only this one wore an impeccable olive-drab uniform, not a red suit, and instead of a white beard, he had a thick red one.

As I later discovered, Piñeiro was a vice minister of the interior and a member of the Central Committee. But his power base was as head of the Americas Department of the Cuban Communist Party, the agency in charge of dealing with Havana's revolutionary projects throughout Latin America. It was created from what had previously been a section of Cuban intelligence, which in turn belonged to the Cuban Ministry of the Interior. As its chief, "Redbeard" Piñeiro possessed his own logistical supplies and intelligence, and he could veto all ambassadorial appointments in Latin America. In other words, he was a *comandante,* wrapped in the prestige that the title conferred.

But when I was a boy, I knew Piñeiro only as the godfather who took my father's place during his long absences. He was concerned about the family's trivial problems, even my troubles in school. On weekends he would take me and his own son (who was my age) to the movies—that is, to the private showings given every Sunday for the children of the elite—or to the beach. When he was busy, his wife, Lorna, an American ballerina whom he had married when he was studying in the United States, was his stand-in.

"Come, here, Masetti. I need to talk to you," he said on that May afternoon.

All the questionable things I had done in the last few days ran through my head: my absences or tardiness at school, and everything else for which I could possibly be reproached. The *comandante*'s solemn attitude, and the fact that he asked me to come into his sparsely furnished office, indicated that this was about something out of the ordinary, perhaps not grave, but certainly important.

Without any preamble, he said that Latin America, as I must know, was struggling against imperialism, and this struggle was a matter of victory or death. I didn't understand why he was explaining this to me, but I listened attentively. I sensed that he was approaching something momentous.

"Your father commanded a guerrilla column in Argentina," Piñeiro said, "and based on reports from comrades who have been arrested and other sources, we have confirmed his death. We still don't know the circumstances. All we know is that he was alone, and that he got lost in the mountains without any possibility of survival."

Piñeiro continued talking, but now I wasn't listening. In my boy's mind, all sorts of images crowded together: my father fighting duels alone against dark-robed furies, hacking his way through the jungle with a machete, or lying on the peak of a mountain, stretched out lifeless under the remorseless sun. I quickly concocted a fantasy that he had not died, but surely some peasant had found and hidden him and he would reappear as suddenly as he had left. I remembered the last time I saw him. It was at my seventh birthday party, and he spent the afternoon with me, buying me a plastic swimming pool as a present. Upon saying goodbye, he announced that he was going to the Soviet Union to take a course. I asked how long he might be gone. "Two or three years," he answered, the last words he ever spoke to me. He became a ghost with my same name, Jorge Ricardo Masetti—

although he was known as "Ricardo," not "Jorge"—and with the same angular body, dark skin and Italian features. The ghost within me.

Eventually I would get to know my father, not as a little boy but as an adult. Even more than for most sons, because of who he was, it would be the work of a lifetime. I would be able to picture him as a journalist arriving in Cuba from Argentina in 1958, climbing into the Sierra Maestra to do a story on the revolutionaries fighting against Fulgencio Batista. He interviewed Fidel and Che, his countryman. He decided to join these guerrillas in the fight against the numerically superior professional army that propped up the Cuban dictatorship.

After spending several months in the Sierra Maestra, he returned to Argentina to write a book about his experience. At the same time, he committed himself fervently to solidarity work on behalf of the bearded Cuban rebels, and while thus engaged he was surprised by the revolutionary triumph on January 1, 1959. Responding to an invitation by the new government, he traveled immediately to Cuba, accompanied by my mother and my sister and me. We arrived on January 8, 1959, the same day that Fidel entered Havana at the climax of a triumphal march across the country newly liberated from the Batista regime.

At first, my father participated in and helped to organize what the Cubans called "Operation Truth." This was an effort to let the world know what was happening in Cuba via channels that bypassed the international press agencies. Later, at Che's request, he dedicated himself with great enthusiasm to the creation and management of the Cuban news agency Prensa Latina. Within a few months it had bureaus in the major capitals of Latin America and the world—Buenos Aires, Mexico City, Rio de Janeiro and others—and was spreading the Cuban word with feverish activity. Journalists and writers of the stature of Gabriel García Márquez, Rodolfo Walsh, Carlos María Gutiérrez and Plínio Apuleyo Mendoza went to Havana to place themselves in the service of the news agency.

But the dreams of these first days were not to endure. The gaze of the ambitious old militants of the Cuban Communist Party, otherwise known as the People's Socialist Party, came to rest on Prensa Latina. Thus began a war for control of this organization. My father presented his resignation in 1961, expecting full backing from Fidel. To his surprise and dismay, the resignation was accepted. His creation, Prensa Latina, was given to others greedy for the power the organization conferred on them.

My father went through a period of disillusionment. Subsequently, he began working with Piñeiro, who made an agent of him—just as he would, in time, make of me. As such, he was sent on a mission to Algeria to assist the National Liberation Front (FLN) in the last phase of its war against the French colonists. Upon returning to Cuba, he remained only long enough to prepare his departure for Argentina, where, at Che Guevara's insistence, he was to head a guerrilla column in the heavily forested northern region. This was the first guerrilla project in which Che was personally involved. But my father was no soldier. His band, weakened by dissension, was probably infiltrated by agents of the Argentine secret police. Perhaps he was betrayed by one of his own.

He never made it out of the mountains. He was killed there, and his body was never recovered.

I SHED NO TEARS WHEN PIÑEIRO told me that my father was dead. I lied to the *comandante,* telling him I already knew what had happened. It was my way of protecting my father, of maintaining a fantasy that I thought would keep him from harm.

"We calculate that it was in April 1964, last year." Piñeiro puffed nervously on his cigar as he dutifully forged ahead. "We don't have all the facts, and for security reasons, we considered it inopportune at that time to inform the family."

I had no idea then of all the things they would conceal from me in the future "for reasons of security."

I ran out of the room. I don't even remember if I said goodbye to Piñeiro. I ran several blocks without stopping. I didn't stop to catch a tadpole in the fountain at the green house, as I normally might have; I didn't throw rocks at the hens of our neighbor Alfonso; nor did I stop in front of Teresita's house to scare her with ghost stories; I needed to get home to tell everything to my mother.

"Mommy, Mommy! Piñeiro told me Papá is dead!" I blurted out as I ran into the kitchen.

I saw then that she already knew. My older sister Graciela, my mother's confidante, also knew. The two of them began to weep. I had been the only one spared my family's pain. Though I had noticed that in the last few weeks my mother seemed very sad, I hadn't stopped to ask myself why. It was usual for her to be sad during my father's absences.

The news was made public a few days later. The government dedicated buildings in my father's name, the newspapers spoke of him in the hushed tones reserved for martyrs, and supposed friends told anecdotes that proved how good a revolutionary he had been. I felt my father's death in my heart, but could not imagine the evil consequences that his legacy would bring me.

Almost immediately, I ceased being called Jorge and became "the son of Masetti."

"Masetti, aren't you ashamed to get such bad grades? What would your father say?" This became the mantra of my teachers.

I was sure that he wouldn't have said anything—that he, too, hated mathematics. But I dared not say so. I was "the son of...." I was expected to be the best in everything.

The consequence was, of course, that for the next few years I did the complete opposite. If long hair was held in disfavor, I wore mine shoulder-length. If tight pants were frowned upon, I wore mine so tight I had to put them on with talcum powder.

In Cuban schools, every classroom bears the name of a hero or martyr of the Revolution. I don't remember what teacher dreamed it up—no doubt a Communist Party militant—but in order to enforce an improvement in my conduct, they named my classroom after my father. But my reaction was not what they hoped for. Not only did I not improve but, in a fit of rage, I tore down the little name sign my teacher had made with such care. They hauled me in front of a disciplinary committee, which punished me for "antisocial behavior with counterrevolutionary tendencies."

I was twelve years old at the time.

I DON'T KNOW WHETHER IT WAS because of depression or neurological problems, or, more likely, because of both, but about this time my mother's health began to deteriorate and she commenced a long odyssey through various psychiatric institutions. She never got over my father, although he had been living with another woman when he left on his fateful mission. My mother developed an uncontrollable persecution complex, a condition so severe that she made my sister and me sleep inside a closet to protect us from imaginary attackers. Finally, the decision was made to commit her to a mental institution.

My sister Graciela and I lived alone or with the women who came to do domestic chores from time to time, whose names I cannot remember. Meanwhile, my mother was interned at a psychiatric center located in the downtown district of Vedado, which was reserved for family members of those connected to the Ministry of the Interior. It was a stately old mansion surrounded by gardens. My sister and I would sit with my mother on benches under the shade of the ceiba trees during the three visits we were allowed each week. The electric shock treatments and the quantities of barbiturates they administered made it hard for her to maintain a coherent conversation. She was barely able to talk, much less speak rationally.

One day they told us we couldn't visit her. We insisted. When Graciela began to scream they finally let us in, after warning us that we should not let ourselves be shocked by what we were about to see. We found my mother tied to her bed, almost unconscious. But she was able to ask us to get her out.

I have never been able to banish that image from my nightmares.

Yet other things were happening that also affected me. This was a time of increasing mobilization as the United States was being knocked around in Southeast Asia. The press, television and wall posters incessantly shouted revolutionary slogans:

"Create two, three, many Vietnams!"

"The first duty of a revolutionary is to make revolution!"

"Make the Andes into the Sierra Maestra of Latin America!"

The guerrillas towered over all the other larger-than-life figures in my generation's childhood games. Cubans followed the development of the guerrilla struggle with passion, as if it were a huge global baseball game. The image of Che was present in Cubans' everyday life, stimulating effort and sacrifice. Even before he met his end in Bolivia, the metamorphosis into myth had begun.

His death in 1967 had a profound impact on me. I remember that during a solemn wake for him, I cried and cried, the tears coming from somewhere deep within. It was Che's death, but the image in my mind was my father's; the wake was his wake, long delayed.

As the slogans took hold, I began to think that despite his short life, my father had managed to achieve a place in history. He was no longer mine alone: he belonged to Cuba. My father's self-sacrifice in the South American forests, a backdrop to Che Guevara's, made him an unquestionable hero. His abandonment of us was not important; he'd had historic responsibilities, after all. To really make a difference and be a man, one had to live and die like him.

I never mentioned these thoughts for fear of seeming self-aggrandizing. Yet my fantasies were not entirely misplaced. Later on I would discover that the guerrilla war my father had tried to spark in Argentina was actually Che's first project for igniting revolution throughout Latin America. He had planned to join my father and take command of the guerrilla column himself once it had been established as a going concern.

My mother's condition worsened and my maternal grandmother came to visit us from Argentina. She couldn't stop lamenting the situation and blaming my father, Che Guevara, Fidel Castro, the devil, or whomever else she could think of for what had befallen her daughter. She went to the Cuban authorities to arrange for our return to Argentina. The answer, of course, was that this could not be easily accomplished "for reasons of security" that were so serious they took priority over my mother's health.

"There is a military government in Argentina," the government officials told us. "It is not opportune to travel at this time. The kids don't have passports and there is no Argentine embassy here in Cuba. In any case, we have to consult about the case at the highest level."

My grandmother's stubborn insistence granted them no respite. Besides talking with every Cuban bureaucrat they put in front of her, she prayed to her pantheon of Catholic saints and to others she had begun to adopt from the Afro-Cuban religion, Santeria. I don't know if it was the prayers or the benevolence of the bureaucratic big shots that caused the obstacles to be removed, but in the end my grandmother got what she wanted. We were informed that we could go home after all.

I felt a strange mixture of fear and joy. On the one hand, there was fear of the unknown and of abandoning the security that Cuba offered; on the other, the chance of returning to my own country and belonging to a family like everyone else—and the dream that, by returning, my mother would recover.

They had taken me to Cuba in January 1959 when I was three.

I returned to Argentina at the age of fourteen.

I left behind my friends, my neighborhood, my first puppy loves, Fidel, Che, Comandante Piñeiro, and my father.

2

BUENOS AIRES, 1970–1971

My arrival in Buenos Aires was not marked by the strong emotional closure I had hoped for. There were the hugs and tears usual among newfound family members, but there was something ominous about the comments people made.

"Jorge, have I ever told you how much you look like your father?" said my good, neurotic Aunt Yolanda, her eyes brimming with tears.

I presented my best deadpan, in keeping with the moment, to avoid giving an answer. But I wasn't sure: was she saying something about my destiny as well as my appearance?

Eventually I ceased to be a novelty. People stopped making these portentous comments, and our life took on a normal rhythm.

In our new habitat, my mother's condition improved; I wondered fleetingly if it was Cuba that had been her sickness. Our life was organized along lines that a true revolutionary would call petit bourgeois. We lived in a small, pretty apartment on Charcas Street. For the time being, my father's family paid our expenses and my sister and I began to study like other children and work in the family business.

I suppose the fact that I was never consulted about the plans they had for me, combined with the usual adolescent rebelliousness, made me systematically reject everything that was suggested to me. Becoming intolerant of my mother and her relapses, I first decided to go live with an uncle, then later with a family friend who studied medicine and belonged to the Argentine Communist Party. The latter was a man of great kindness, for whom I never ceased being a curiosity because I had been raised in a real socialist country. Under his influence, I began to justify my rebellious attitude as a rejection of capitalism.

Reading became my refuge. I was particularly taken by Herman Hesse's *Steppenwolf,* identifying with the solitary protagonist. At night, I would wander along Corrientes Street, from one bookstore to another, concentrating on observing the various types I saw there—some with a conspiratorial air as if hiding something important; others marginal people or provincials recently arrived in the city, wasting their time as cheaply as possible. I loved the bohemian atmosphere.

The Buenos Aires I saw on those nocturnal strolls always seemed to me like an old prostitute who once upon a time was beautiful, but after too many late nights is left only with her makeup—a grotesque caricature of what she once was, but still able to charm.

My life was cafés, books, walking around, and trying on and discarding various selves. Then I met Lucía.

I was in the habit of going every night to a little café that stood between Florida and Corrientes Streets, in the heart of Buenos Aires. It was not especially nice, but it was cheap, and they kept a bottle of atrocious cognac on the counter that you could drink for free. There was also a juke box with excellent music, and I listened with the affected pose of a melancholy ruffian, as if pondering transcendent matters.

I had a well-developed sense of smell. (My friends never missed an opportunity to say that this was perhaps due to the size of my nose.) One day, I was overwhelmed by the heady perfume emanating from a stunning girl with a mop of chestnut hair. She was wearing a white dress down to her ankles, and possessed eyes that would have defeated even the most valiant warrior.

This goddess was chatting with a grimy, skinny guy whom I immediately hated. When she left, I paid for my coffee, the only thing I had consumed in the four hours or so that I spent there, and followed her.

She took Corrientes Street toward the obelisk. She stopped in front of a shop window; I also stopped, maintaining the distance between us. She continued walking and I followed. After passing July 9 Avenue, she went into the Ramos café, an old, traditional establishment with marble tables. She ordered a gin. I sat at the table next to her and asked for a mineral water, the cheapest item on the menu. Racking my brain to figure out how to approach her, I became so absorbed in my fantasy of seduction that she almost escaped. Fortunately, to exit she had to bump into my table. This roused me and I rushed out after her. At the intersection with Callao Street she stopped. I stopped too and stood like a lamppost.

She regarded me contemptuously and said: "What on earth are you doing, following me like a crazy man for over half an hour?"

If any motorist had seen me at that moment, he would have slammed on the brakes, mistaking my face for the red light.

"I think I know you," I babbled.

This response was so completely unoriginal that she began to laugh. My confusion must have seemed life-threatening. She took pity on me and invited me for a cup of coffee. I didn't know what to do—I had spent my last change on that mineral water at the Ramos.

"I don't have a cent," I finally admitted, wishing that the earth would swallow me up.

"No matter," she said. "I'll pay."

From then on, things went so well, it was as if Providence itself had arranged them.

She was nineteen, three years older than I. She had been studying sociology, but she was not attending classes at present because she was working and saving her money to go to Brazil. For my part, I lied shamelessly. I told her that I was eighteen and that next year I would begin my studies in history. I don't know how many gins we drank or how long we talked, but I do know that it was a lot of gin and we talked about everything.

She found it amusing that I had grown up in Cuba and she began to call me "Little Cuban."

We left the bar around four in the morning. I offered to walk her home. She lived at the corner of Juncal and Junín, about ten blocks from the place where we met. Daringly, I took her hand. She didn't pull away. At this point I was completely in love and dreaming of living with her the rest of my life.

When we got to her place, she asked if I wanted to come up and smoke marijuana. I had never done this before, but I certainly knew what marijuana was. I said, "Of course."

Her apartment was tiny but comfortable. In one space she had the bed, a corner with a pile of pillows on the floor. There was a bookcase built of planks on glass bricks, a Winco record player, and on the wall, sure enough, among the images of longhaired rock singers, a photo of Che.

Inexperience paralyzed me, and fear of seeming stupid made me feel even stupider than I actually was.

"Roll one while I go to the bathroom," she said, passing me a bag with the weed and a packet of rolling papers.

I don't know whether it was my nerves or my total ignorance of the subject, but it was impossible for me to roll that joint. My clumsiness was embarrassing, so I put on a record and stretched out on the pillows, trying out a few poses that might suggest confidence. I listened to the steady rush of water in the shower.

When she came out, her hair was wet and she was completely naked. She moved with such unaffected naturalness that at first I didn't even feel aroused. She sat down next to me and rolled the joint with the facility of a tobacco-rollin' cowboy in a Western movie.

After smoking, we sat smiling at each other a long time. She extended her hand and began to caress my face gently, barely touching, as if trying to recognize me in the dark. I was floating. My body exuded an intense and agreeable heat.

She took me by the hand and brought me to bed. We made love, or, more precisely, she made love to me. When I woke up, I couldn't quite fathom where I was. Then I saw her, reading among the pillows. I realized it had not been a dream.

"Are you happy?" she asked me, smiling.

In that moment, what could I answer? I felt like Che Guevara, Jim Morrison, Fidel Castro, Napoleon Bonaparte—all of them rolled together. In an attack of honesty, I confessed that it was the first time I had made love, that I had never smoked marijuana before, and that actually I was only sixteen. She smiled, playing with my hair and calling me her Little Lying Cuban.

LUCÍA BECAME MY LOVER, MY FRIEND, my sidekick. She had a very complex relationship with her parents. They were rich and gave her everything except affection. Sociology didn't interest her, but she studied it just to annoy her father, who, as a military man, considered this subject leftist and inconsequential. We laughed when we thought about the expression on his face should he find out that his daughter was going out with the son of a Cuban guerrilla who had died fighting the Argentine status quo.

Lucía taught me the secrets of sex and I made every effort to be a model student. We liked to make love in risky places: in parks, in entrance halls, even behind the back of a guard in the early morning train we took all the way to La Plata. We smoked marijuana in every corner of the town. We tried to get to the edge, to be provocative, to live dangerously. I became an expert on grass, learning where to buy it, how to recognize its quality by its color, and how to avoid being cheated on price. (I discovered that the grimy, skinny guy I hated so much when I first saw Lucía was nothing more than her drug connection.) I installed myself in her house with my toothbrush and the rest of my belongings

One of the games we liked best was to sit facing each other, with paper and pencil, and write down the words that were passing through our minds, alternating hers with mine to create a text. The result was crazy, but the effects of the marijuana inevitably made it seem profound.

One night when, as she used to say, Lucía was obliged to disguise herself as a bourgeois lady in order to dine with her parents and get the money that made possible a life of pleasure, I grabbed the opportunity for a marijuana sortie. I made my rounds to various bars in Corrientes Street, but couldn't find any of my contacts. I took the subway to the Carlos Pellegrini station and got out at Primera Junta, searching for a dealer among the shadows. In an old, smoke-filled bar I found the grimy, skinny guy. The place was as dirty and rundown as he was. I signaled to him and we went out; I bought only enough for two or three joints, because I didn't have money for more.

I had gone barely fifty meters when two plainclothes police arrested me. They were narcotics agents and, as soon as they found the little packet I had just bought, they shoved me with a kick and a curse into their car and took me to the station. There I was practically lifted into the air and tossed into a jail cell as grim as jails all over the world must be.

What struck me most were the desperate, crazed inscriptions on the gray walls:

HERE SUFFERS A MAN BUT HE KEEPS SILENT

MAMA, FORGIVE ME

I GOT BUSTED BECAUSE I'M A FOOL

For several hours they left me there without telling me anything. My fear grew. Around two in the morning they came for me and took me to the office of the police commissioner, an oily fat guy with a drunk's red nose. He was wearing an impeccable gray suit that was too short for him; you could see his socks flowing into his shiny shoes. For a while he left me standing in the middle of the room while he circled around me making faces like a rabid dog; all that was lacking was foam at the corners of his mouth.

"So you're the 'Little Cuban,' eh?" he said, throwing the first punch.

Little Cuban? I thought as I recoiled from the blow. *That's what Lucía calls me.* And how could the creepy son of a bitch know that?

So many things flashed through my mind that I hardly felt the punches that followed. Who had informed on me?

Winding up the first barrage of kicks and blows, they sat me down at a table and commenced the interrogation.

"Who sells you the grass? Where is the girl who always goes around with you?"

They questioned me with manic intensity, never giving me a moment to respond. I tried to convey to them that I had no idea what they were talking about, that the packet they had found on me was a gift from a guy I had never met before, and that I couldn't say what girl they were talking about because I always went out with different ones.

Again a blizzard of blows and questions; again I gave the same answers.

After this routine had been repeated several times, one of the cops went out and came back in with the grimy, skinny guy. To see him planted in front of me was even worse than the physical punishment I had taken: my whole story had collapsed.

This is the guy who ratted on me, I thought. But strangely, I felt a certain compassion, thinking they must have beaten him up too.

Then I saw him bantering quite naturally with the police. And soon he joined in on the interrogation, throwing a few punches of his own. Only then did I understand that this ugly bastard was one of those pipsqueak dealers employed by the police as a blackmailed informant in their undercover work.

I swore to the cops that he was my sole supplier. I mentioned Lucía by an alias and assured them I didn't know where she lived, and that we met only in the bars on Corrientes.

They put me back in the cell. I was exhausted and in excruciating pain. An absurd part of the situation was that I actually felt fortunate—I had merely been beaten, not tortured. I knew very well what torture was: the repeated dunkings in water, electric shocks, burning with cigarettes and other systematic cruelties reserved, for the most part, for political prisoners. But I was a minor, and by law they had to put me before a juvenile court within twenty-four hours, which limited the amount and kind of punishment they could dish out.

They took me to the detention center for young delinquents in a patrol car. As soon as they opened the enormous gates, I knew what awaited me. After filling out routine forms, I was locked up in the hole where I would stay for the next two months: a dark gray cell with a mattress on the floor and a torn and dirty yellow blanket. During the day, the bars remained open and I was free to go out into the yard and play soccer—or simply walk around and talk with the other prisoners. The food was frightful, the jailors worse.

Visits were on Sunday. I felt sure no one would ever find me. But one day when I was sitting in the waiting room, I saw the bald head of my uncle Adolfo, my mother's brother. Contrary to what I expected, he did not challenge me or ask for explanations. He even laughed, and told me not to worry because he had spoken with the judge and found out they were charging me only with consumption and not selling, which made the situation far less serious. His attitude cheered me up.

The days grew longer. My hatred for that foul place grew more and more intense. Anxiously I awaited my appointment with the judge. Meanwhile, I waged an implacable campaign against an invasion of bedbugs into my mattress.

Finally, they granted me my long-awaited liberty. I was left at the disposition of the juvenile court, which ordered me to live in my mother's house. Naturally, the first thing I did after being released was to go to Lucía's house.

I didn't find her. I returned two hours later and still she wasn't there.

The third time, I encountered the housekeeper in the entryway.

"The señorita from the fifth floor has gone to Brazil," she said while she mopped the floor with a wet rag.

I never found out if Lucía knew of my arrest.

3
Buenos Aires, 1972–1973

MISTREATMENT AT THE HANDS of the police and those weeks in the reformatory changed my life. I was not willing to be arrested again for such a trifle. I decided that if I were ever to go to jail again it would be for something big.

At the end of 1972, Argentina was going through a revolutionary upsurge from which it was impossible to remain aloof. You could read about the deeds of the guerrilla organizations every day in the press, especially the Montoneros, a left faction of the Peronist Youth Movement, and the People's Revolutionary Army (known by its Spanish initials, ERP), a Cuban-inspired group. There were serious doctrinal differences between them, but in the mind of the people, both were simply against the government, and together they dominated the headlines of the principal newspapers. I doubt if there was a young person in Argentina who was not galvanized by the stories of revolutionary struggle.

I began to work as an apprentice hack for a local newspaper—covering the police beat. My boss was a veteran journalist who knew all the tricks of the trade. He sent me out into the streets to gather information. When I came back with something, he made me write it over and over until it was fit to print.

While I was covering the crime scene, I was also trying to make contact with one of the guerrilla organizations, with no particular preference for any one. In fact, I had no idea what their political agendas were, and I had not formed an agenda of my own. My position—to put it rather baldly—was simply romantic. Che Guevara, the struggle for justice, hatred of the police and the military: these were the foundations of my politics.

Someone put me in touch with a female psychologist who had known one of the *compañeros* that had fought with my father's guerrilla column. She in turn introduced me to him. Thus did I come to know Jorge Belomo, a man of thirty years or so, somewhat short, with a short man's vitality. He was very agile in his movements and he spoke as confidently as he moved, but his very energy made him seem somewhat brusque. He did not identify himself politically, but clearly he was a militant and deeply committed to some cause. That at least is the impression I received from the deference shown him by the other *compañeros* the first day I talked to him. Striking a conspiratorial pose, I suggested to him that we meet again.

Two or three days later, we met in the Café Violetas, at the corner of Rivadavia and Medrano streets; it was an old-fashioned patisserie, of which a few still remained in the Buenos Aires of the early 1970s. We got right to the point. Jorge spoke about politics: how, as a result of the guerrillas' daring, the Argentine military was now on the defensive. For my part, I told him that I wanted to link up with the guerrilla movement and hoped he would be the link.

In fact, Belomo was a leader of the People's Revolutionary Army–22nd of August, which had split off from the ERP because it supported Peronism in the elections of March 1973. To be truthful, I couldn't care less about any of these matters; I was simply glad to be involved at last with real guerrillas.

I could no longer call Belomo by his real name. I was informed that from then on, he would be known as "Herman." I also had to find myself a pseudonym, so I baptized myself "Emilio." About one week later, we met again in the Plaza Flores so he could introduce me to other *compañeros.* I got into his car and he handed me some dark glasses, lined on the inside with black cloth. He explained that I must not be able to identify the house where the meeting would take place. All this mysteriousness excited me, and convinced me that I would be participating in important affairs.

We arrived at our destination. Inside, I took off the glasses and saw a small, modestly furnished apartment. The drawn blinds prevented me from seeing outside. The rest of the *compañeros* were already there. Introductions were made: Ariel, Chango, Moni and I, Emilio— all noms de guerre. It was hard for me that first time to introduce myself with a name that was not my own. As the years went by, the reverse would happen and I would feel strange telling someone I was Jorge. Nonetheless I had a strong feeling that I had now begun my clandestine life, with a baptism into its names, rules, codes and—above all—myths.

We sat at a round table. It was clear that Herman was the highest-ranking member of the group because of the respectful way the others addressed him. He told them that I would work with them for a while to familiarize myself with the organization's political line, and that later they would decide what front I would be sent to. Then, with great solemnity, we moved on to the rest of the agenda: the national situation, the international situation, the group's finances, and our various tasks.

Puffing cigarettes and sipping maté, the herbal, slightly caffeinated tea that Argentines like to drink from round cups, the men carefully debated each point. I listened with great interest. When we came to the mission at hand, I realized that this cell was a propaganda team. We were supposed to paint slogans about the organization and its policy in a certain area of Buenos Aires. We were also supposed to distribute the party newspaper and, since we needed weapons and procuring them was a shared responsibility, plan the disarming of a few policemen. This last project interested me the most: I was finally and without delay going to see some real action, even though I had never held a weapon in my hands except for the B.B. gun I was given as a boy, with which I used to terrorize the neighborhood sparrows.

To my great joy, Herman took out a fine-looking pistol from his suit jacket, showed me how to take it apart and put it back together again, and told me how to fire it. It was a 9 mm Browning; on it was the seal of the Federal Police. No doubt it had been "expropriated," which made it doubly attractive. He told me I had to learn to disassemble and reassemble it with my eyes blindfolded. Meanwhile, the other *compañeros* practiced shooting blanks.

That's the way nearly all the meetings went: one period devoted to politics, the other to military preparation.

Who could have divined in those days of euphoria and triumphalism what destiny held in store for all of us there? Herman (Jorge Belomo) was murdered in 1975 by the Argentine Anticommunist Alliance, or Triple-A, a death squad that blew him up with a car bomb; Ariel and his companion Moni (Daniel Hopen and Monica Carreira) were kidnapped after the military coup of March 1976, adding their names to the already long list of the disappeared; I never heard what happened to Chango.

I didn't know it then, but I had just stepped into a tunnel of death.

I continued to work at the newspaper, but it was now my cover rather than my occupation. Events and the dynamic of Argentine politics determined our group's activities. I stole weapons, wrote pamphlets, or painted graffiti slogans almost every day. On one mission the police surprised us, and I had my first experience of armed confrontation. We had posted a sentinel at each corner, and one of them gave the alert, repositioning himself to open fire. We had a fallback plan, according to which we were supposed to withdraw in an alternating fashion, each covering another. In the event, I was so confused I didn't even know which way to shoot. I glimpsed the profiles of two cops and in less than a minute I had shot off an entire clip of thirteen rounds. Fortunately, our team included more experienced *compañeros* and we carried out the retreat without taking casualties. I can't deny I was afraid, but afterward I was euphoric—the feeling I imagine parachutists enjoy after making their first jump.

From that moment on, I put armed struggle ahead of any other revolutionary activity, and the disdain I felt toward legal political work or mass organizing was so absolute that I considered it a punishment to carry out such duties at all.

As I FORGED MY NEW IDENTITY, the ghost of my father became more insistent. Occasionally, I even went so far as to write him letters, as if he were still alive. Here is one of them I have kept from early 1973:

> Dear Papá:
>
> You can't imagine how much I miss you. There are so many things I wish I could ask you about. Finally, I feel as if I am beginning to be worthy of you, even though I have a long way to go. Sometimes I think that the enterprise I am beginning today isn't big enough, but in any case, for now I have no alternative and you have to start somewhere.
>
> The *compañeros* are good, and show signs of great dedication, though I think a lot of time gets wasted in theoretical sessions that don't get us anywhere. It's possible I'm wrong, since I am just beginning.
>
> Sometimes I am afraid on operations. I can confess this to you only because I know you understand me. Any weakness is interpreted as a failure of revolutionary nerve, or petit bourgeois mentality. Imagine: I can't even tell them about my relationship with Lucía because of that mess with the pot. If they were to find out, I think they would expel me. I'm sure that many of them have done the same. It's a fact of life in our generation. I don't understand what sort of prejudice leads them to construct such moral myths,

but sometimes I have the feeling that I'm surrounded by monks. In spite of this, their principles and objectives are very noble.

It is very hard for me to have to go around concealing my personal history, above all because the *compañeros* who know that I was in Cuba and that I am your son idealize me a lot and expect much of me. I hope not to let them down, and not to let you and the Cuban Revolution down. If I hadn't been so immature and undisciplined, I could have learned much more from the Revolution, and I would have been more useful.

Now I understand more clearly why you almost never had time to be with me and at the end abandoned me. As a boy, I tell you now, I suffered a lot because of your absence. Of course, it was difficult then for me to understand that the Revolution is much more important than any of us and that it requires we renounce even those we love.

Poor Mamá, she could never understand this and she got sick because of it, and she is still very ill. Without knowing why, she found herself far from her family, her friends, her original environment—and above all, she lost you.

I promise you I will keep moving ahead.

I love you very much.

Your son,

Jorge

Despite pressure from my revolutionary comrades, who wanted me to move to the political or labor section, I stayed on the police beat for my newspaper. But I had lost interest in journalism. All I wanted was to become a member of a military squad, and I dedicated most of my time to that goal.

The Urban Guerrilla's Mini-Manual, by the Brazilian Carlos Marighela; *What Every Revolutionary Should Know about Political Repression,* by Victor Serge; and *The Tupamaro Files*—these manuals became my bedtime reading, along with *Chronicles of the Revolutionary War,* by Che Guevara. I even read Menachem *Begin's Rebellion in the Holy Land.* I must have studied Costa-Gavras's *State of Siege* five or six times. I devoured everything that came into my hands concerning the military methodology of waging revolution.

The elections of March 11, 1973, gave the Peronist party a victory over the Radical Party. President Salvador Allende of Chile and figurehead President Osvaldo Dorticos of Cuba attended Perón's inaugural ceremonies. That same day, within the framework of a great popular mobilization, the political prisoners were freed. It was time for a great revolutionary fiesta.

"Chile! Cuba! The people salute you!"

"Perón! Evita! The fatherland is socialist."

Argentina could then boast the most democratic government in its history, but the time of celebration lasted only forty-five days. The contradictions within Peronism, a revolutionary movement containing both left-wing and right-wing elements, grew apace. Soon both sides were letting their weapons do the talking.

Perón, the movement's old caudillo, turned his back with particular vehemence on our band of revolutionary young people who had supported him and helped him return to his country after an exile of eighteen years. In a great political maneuver, he called new elections and, by an overwhelming majority, was returned to power with an almost fascist program granting vastly increased muscle to the most extreme Peronist factions.

Initially, I too had joined in the general enthusiasm. But as the situation deteriorated, I finally contrived my switch into the military structure of our organization. For the time being, we limited ourselves to a few propaganda actions and shooting up some right-wing Peronists' offices. We couldn't act more forcefully because we were still more or less Peronists and still more or less Marxists, which is to say we were nothing much at all.

The People's Revolutionary Army (ERP), on the other hand, knew what it was up to. It had declared war on imperialist businesses and on the military, carrying out spectacular actions at a much more intense rate than any other Argentine revolutionary organization. In their speeches, they always referred to Che and to the protracted war. I identified more and more with this discourse. So I quit the 22nd of August faction and joined the main wing of the ERP.

I found that they were even more austere in their monkish devotion to the cause than our splinter group had been. To gain entry into their organization you first had to pass what they called a "short initiation course," designed to deepen your understanding of their party line. Weapons-handling ability was required. A text called "Morality and Proletarianization" was a kind of bible intended to govern our intimate life and rid us of any residues of bourgeois longings. It went so far as to indicate how we should educate our children:

> The raising of children is a common task of the couple, and not only of the couple, but of the group of *compañeros* who share the home. In this regard, we must actively promote a new attitude. When we speak of sharing in the communal living places, we refer not only to political-military activity but also to study, the utiliza-

tion of free time, and the common tasks of daily life. These tasks must include the raising of the children who share the same house.

I was ordered to look for work in a factory and go live in an "operational house," a sort of revolutionary commune. At the time, I had already started a relationship with a *compañera,* Mónica, who was the leader of the cell. At twenty-seven she was older than I. She was thin and intense, a highly disciplined and intellectually committed person who usually dressed in jeans and running shoes, the uniform of the Argentine leftist. We lived with another couple, and together we formed an "agitation and propaganda" cell. Our work consisted of carrying out armed propaganda missions and distributing the party newspaper in factories and other places.

I must confess that the life of the revolutionary was initially unbearable to me because we were required to discuss our most intimate problems in the collective self-criticism sessions. I quickly learned to keep my mouth shut during these sessions, because once you revealed some crevice in your personality, your comrades bored in. The only thing that gave me pleasure was planning the operations we were assigned to carry out. But even here my sense of discipline, as the organization viewed it, was far from exemplary. I was often punished for my impulsiveness. Monica, though much more disciplined than I, also paid a price because she was unable to change my behavior.

Partly as a result of my frustration with the regimen imposed on me, I made contact with the Cuban embassy, where initially I had gone in search of letters from my family and friends left behind on the island. In one of the meetings with the Cuban official with whom I had regular contact, I was told that my boyhood mentor Comandante Piñeiro wanted me to visit Cuba so I could witness the advances the Revolution had made in the years I had been away. He also said that I would be able to undergo military training.

I returned from the embassy in an excellent mood and told Monica. She also had big news: she was going to have a child. My next thought was that it would be better if she, too, went to Cuba so that the child would be born under socialism.

At first, the organization was wary about the invitation because it had not been made through the party, but to me personally. But in the end, using my influence with one of the *compañeros* who liked me a lot and was close to the leaders, I got my way: I would travel first and Monica would come later.

In November 1974, I once again left Argentina for Cuba.

I wasn't yet twenty years old. But the fact that I was going to receive military instruction, combined with the child we were expecting, made me feel like a man.

FLIGHTS FROM ARGENTINA TO CUBA were not direct, but involved a stopover in Lima, Peru. I was told that an official from the Cuban embassy would meet me at the Lima airport and that I would stay in the city for forty-eight hours before continuing on to Havana. When I met him, he asked if I had somewhere to stay for the night. I knew no one in Lima, and everything to do with travel and airports was foreign to me. So he took me to the Hotel Crillon and gave me $300 for my expenses. This was a huge amount of money—far more than the monthly budget of the *compañeros* back home.

After the layover, I left for Havana on a Cubana Airlines flight. On board, I already breathed a different air. The nonchalance of the flight attendants, the strident voices of the Cuban passengers, and the warm beer made me feel that I was coming home. My heart lifted when the voice of the flight attendant came over the intercom at the end of the flight: "In a few minutes we will be landing at José Martí International Airport in Havana, Cuba, the first socialist country in the Americas. Please fasten your seatbelts."

Disembarking, I rejoiced in the sticky heat of the Caribbean and the scent of the ocean. The colors, the smells ... everything was familiar to me.

At the foot of the stairway an official with a neatly pressed *guayabera* shirt and a cigar in his hand greeted me with a smile and asked me to accompany him to the VIP lounge. Someone would take care of getting my bags through customs. After I had waited a while in the luxurious surroundings of the lounge, the official reappeared with his impeccable bureaucrat's smile to say, "Everything is all worked out." Without realizing it, I had just entered the world of "important people"—the nomenklatura.

Conchita, the woman who lived with my father after he had separated from my mother, was waiting for me at the exit. She was a charming, plump little woman who worked for the Ministry of the Interior. It amused me that they had sent her to pick me up on account of a presumed personal connection, when in fact we had never even met. At first both of us felt uncomfortable. But gradually our relationship got past all the bureaucratic formalism. Thanks to Conchita, I was able to get a clearer picture of my father. She told me forgotten details, anecdotes that I did not know. Through her I also met my half-sister Laura, whom I had heard about but knew only as one of the family secrets that could not be mentioned because of my mother's illness. I discovered with surprise that she looked a lot like me—even more so than my full sister, Graciela. Later on, Laura confided to me that when we first met, I amounted to little more for her than just another stranger dressed in a ridiculous maroon suit that was too small for him.

They put me up in the Capri Hotel in Vedado, one of the elegant hotels of old Havana whose pre-Revolution owner had been the well-known actor and gangster George Raft. They registered me under a false name, José Fernandez Serruti, and assigned me a Costa Rican nationality, all of which seemed pretty ridiculous to me since many people in Havana already knew me and my family. It was my first experience of Cuban security's mania for playing spy games and complicating things that should be straightforward.

They gave me a charge card that was like a magic key to the good life. With the card I could eat all I wanted anywhere in the hotel: the restaurant, the cafeteria, the cabaret. I didn't have to do anything more than sign my name, or more correctly, the name of José Fernandez Serruti. I tried to be careful not to consume more than was necessary. I knew there were shortages in Cuba and that the Cubans were forbidden the delicacies to which I had access. What surprised me was how the party officials who were assigned to me took advantage of the situation. They too had the magic card, with the same last name that appeared on mine, and it was not unusual to see them living it up in the bar or cabaret and charging everything to Luis Fernandez Serruti, who was, I suppose, my fictional persona's fictional brother.

4
Cuba, 1974–1976

The official responsible for me introduced himself as "Morejón." This was the first of many pseudonyms by which I would know him over the years. Thin, but with an enormous double chin and unusually light skin, Morejón was very serious, an anomaly for a Cuban. During the many years I knew him, I never heard him tell a joke.

Reciting at length every Fidel Castro speech that he knew during one of our first meetings, he asked me to be available because "the boss," as he called Comandante Piñeiro, wanted to see me soon. This meant that I could not leave my hotel room. Though I suspected that the meeting might not happen immediately, I never imagined that I was going to remain shut in for almost three days, awaiting the phone call. I was tired and bored and just about to give up and go to my new sister's house when the phone finally rang. It was Piñeiro's driver, saying that he would come by to get me in fifteen minutes. After about two hours, a tall mulatto showed up with the excuse that "the boss" had been very busy but now, finally, could receive me. I later realized that the wait I had been forced to endure was tactical—to make clear who was in charge and make me aware of my dependency, because while I was waiting, I had had to consult with the party apparatus over even the smallest details, such as a request for toothpaste.

We traveled though the Fifth Avenue tunnel and continued on Eighteenth Street until we came to Piñeiro's house. We pulled up the sloping driveway and parked in the garage. The mulatto then led me to the very same office where Piñeiro had told me of my father's death. He offered me coffee and told me to wait; the *comandante* would be arriving shortly.

It was about three in the afternoon. As I waited, I recalled the conversation from nine years earlier. I imagined the pride my father would feel if he could see me now, a proven revolutionary talking with a *comandante* about "business," as he himself had surely done before departing for Argentina. I tried to imagine how many secrets and conspiracies had been hatched in that office. Absorbed in my meditations, I almost didn't notice Piñeiro enter. To all appearances he had just gotten out of bed and taken a shower. His red beard was starting to whiten and he was much thinner and paler. Someone had told me that he had recently suffered a heart attack, but in spite of that he looked pretty healthy to me.

He greeted me effusively and, after some pleasantries about my family, got down to business. He made it clear that in selecting me for the military training course he was making an exception, because now that Cuba had renewed diplomatic relations with Argentina, it was necessary to be very careful in dealing with nationals of that country. But taking into account who my father had been, and the fact that I was almost Cuban, he felt they could justify the risk. If I was in agreement, of course.

That last qualifier struck me as almost absurd. My mouth was watering.

He moved on to political considerations: particularly his concern over the ERP's position on the Peronists, whom he saw as a mass movement that had within it progressive revolutionary elements which could not be ignored. He also seemed worried because a few months earlier the ERP, together with the Tupamaros of Uruguay, the Chilean MIR, and the ELN of Bolivia had joined to form a Revolutionary Coordination Committee to coordinate the various revolutionary efforts of the continent.* According to the Cubans, such coordination should exist and even grow, but in secret, because otherwise it would give Yankee imperialism reason to intervene indiscriminately in any country of the region and reinforce collaboration among the various repressive agencies of the Southern Cone.

---

*The Tupamaros were the "heroes" in the famous French film *State of Seige*. This organization had provoked the Uruguayan military into overthrowing one of the oldest democracies in South America. The MIR (*Movimiento de la Izquierda Revolucionaria*, or Movement of the Revolutionary Left) was close to Fidel. The ELN was founded by Che in Bolivia and was still led at this time by the remnants of his organization there.

Although I maintained a respectful silence, I felt that the Coordination Committee should be public; our policy of turning the struggle into a continental one should be known to the people, and we should not disguise our aims. Turning a revolutionary organization into an intelligence apparatus might guarantee its survival but at the cost of its political growth among the masses, which I believed was its most sacred commitment. But I did not mention any of this because I didn't want anything to interfere with the military training course. I left Piñeiro with the sense that he would continue to be my patron, though always at his own chosen speed.

After two more months of waiting in Havana, Morejón finally put me in contact with the officer who would coordinate the training. He introduced me to Román, a green-eyed mulatto who looked more like one of those tropical musicians from a 1950s Hollywood movie than an operations officer of the Special Troops. Román explained the fundamental outline of the course. I would spend three months in a special military unit called Punto Cero (Point Zero). Because I was on a fast track, I would train alone, even though *compañeros* sent by the various organizations on the continent were usually formed into groups. I would receive instruction in urban operations, marksmanship, self-defense and assault.

Román himself took me to the military unit and there he introduced me to the headquarters staff. They gave me boots, an olive-drab uniform and underwear of the same color. They told me I could not leave the camp for the three months that the course lasted, and that my movements should be limited to a fifty-meter zone around the area to which I was assigned. I could have contact only with the instructors, the political officer who would attend me, and the personnel who brought me my food. If anyone from outside the unit should appear, I was to arrest him and shoot my gun into the air to warn the officer on duty.

Then they put me in the back of a canvas-covered jeep, ensuring that I could not observe the areas through which we would pass, and took off. We finally arrived at our destination, known as Area 36. This was a hilltop, surrounded by heavy forest, where three small buildings had been constructed. One served as a dormitory, one as a classroom, and the other, about thirty meters away, as a dining hall and meeting room. The latter two had open sides and roofs supported by posts, which made it possible to contemplate the magnificent view. From the back of the hill you could even catch a glimpse of the ocean.

The first afternoon, only the political officer came up to see me. He was a nice old guy they called Sanjurjo. He spent a long time telling me about the discipline that one needed to maintain at the camp and the policies of the Cuban Revolution. Later, with a certain nostalgia, he would regale me with a thousand anecdotes about his life as a clandestine militant of the People's Socialist Party, as the old Cuban Communist Party was known before the revolutionary triumph.

"Just so you won't get bored, I've brought you a few books," he said.

Then he said goodbye, leaving behind Lenin's *Military Works*, Engels' *Anti-Duehring*, and *On War* by Clausewitz.

As night fell, I listened to the intense concert of crickets and the calls of the *jutiás*, the ratlike animals that live in hollow trees and emit a sound very much like human whistling. A little later they brought up dinner, which to my Argentine taste was not very appetizing: white rice, black beans, some pieces of very tough boiled meat, and yucca—a tuber with a taste like wax that Cubans love.

After eating and washing up the dishes, I became depressed by my solitude. Listening to the crickets, I thought of Mónica, who had arrived in Havana a few days earlier. The thought of reading the books Sanjurjo had brought gave me a headache. I kept telling myself that I was a man of action who shouldn't have to read at all. I had thought that I would be with other *compañeros*, not entirely alone. But then I told myself that if this was what it took to get military training, I had to get used to it. After a struggle to hang up the mosquito netting, I went to bed fully dressed and let sleep take me.

I was awakened at six in the morning by the sound of a vehicle. Through the window I saw an enormous black man dressed in a karate tunic getting out of a jeep. I was glad I had gone to bed fully dressed. Otherwise he would have known how late I had slept.

The man introduced himself as my self-defense trainer. He told me to take off my uniform and put on short pants and an undershirt, as well as two pairs of socks, because the boots were new and I might get blisters. Being rather thin, and now wearing an undershirt with short pants that were way too big for me and military boots, I must have cut a grotesque figure. I felt that the instructor was looking at me with a certain disappointment. He must have been thinking that he had his work cut out for him.

We did a few calisthenics, and then began running. I don't know how many laps we did around the assigned course. All I remember is that I never stopped cursing myself for all the cigarettes I had smoked in my life. And every time I stepped on a stone, it felt like a burning iron on my heel. Despite my two pairs of socks, the boots were wreaking havoc. When I felt about ready to throw up, my instructor told me to pick up the pace and swing my arms and breathe deeply.

After these warm-ups, I had to do pushups, sit-ups, pull-ups, and I don't know how many other exercises for an hour. Finally, my trainer said we were done for the day and we would start the actual self-defense practice when I was in better shape.

Taking off my socks was torture. When I finished getting dressed, they brought me breakfast: a piece of bread and butter, a huge jar of coffee and another of milk.

At nine, the shooting instructor showed up. After introducing himself as Ernesto, he asked me to help him get the weapons out of his pickup truck. When I saw what he had, I almost went crazy with joy. In all my life I had never seen so much hardware in one place: pistols, revolvers, rifles, submachine guns, heavy machine guns, grenades and even bazookas and rocket launchers, plus a ton of ammunition.

Ernesto was really nice—young, with an easy smile and an attractive innocence. He told me passionately of his desire to fight for the liberation of other peoples, and how he had adopted his pseudonym in honor of Che Guevara, whose given name was also Ernesto. He admitted this last fact with a certain chagrin, noting that, of course, he could never expect to be Che's equal. Perhaps this second Ernesto did show some courage in Angola, Ethiopia, Nicaragua, or some other battlefield to which his life as a revolutionary soldier eventually took him. I don't know. After the course, I never saw him again.

My weapons training began with theory: tactics, effective range, assembly and disassembly, ballistics, and other questions related to the subject. This occupied us for about a week before I got to the shooting range. Meanwhile, Ernesto left me to practice taking apart and putting back together various weapons after he had scrambled the pieces. I had to budget my time so as to do it as quickly as possible. The exercises made my moments alone less boring.

My days took on a predictable rhythm. My body didn't hurt as much as it had the first few sessions with the black guy, and I began self-defense. I went to the range with Ernesto and shot every kind of infantry weapon. We also practiced shooting on the move, defending from attack, on foot and in a car—even shooting a rifle from a small airplane.

One night, at about three in the morning, I was awakened suddenly by yelling.

"Get dressed, get dressed, we are going on maneuvers!" A little man I had never seen before was standing over my cot shouting in my face.

If I hadn't seen the winged parachute insignia above his left breast pocket indicating he was from the Special Troops, I would have thought that an unauthorized crazy person had invaded my sleep. He told me to come out with my equipment, which consisted of a backpack with a blanket, mosquito net, nylon sheet, rope, canteen, rifle, and a web belt with a pistol and cartridges.

We walked toward a road where some other men were in a line waiting for us. He ordered us not to speak among ourselves and to keep five meters apart. After two more stops, where first three and then five more *compañeros* joined up with us, he counted us and explained that we were going on a routine nighttime hike to familiarize ourselves with the terrain. He separated us into three groups: vanguard, center, rearguard.

"Step lively and look ahead. Don't change the pace!" He shouted constantly as he moved with admirable agility from the vanguard to the rearguard and back again.

We were almost falling over one another, tripping on everything we found in our way. It was a moonless night and you couldn't see anything.

The worst part was when we were walking along a railroad bridge, and suddenly we could see the lights of a train in the distance. We were warned to jump off the bridge, because no one was supposed to see us. I don't know how many meters I rolled. I still remember my rifle banging against my side. I can't understand how I kept from fracturing a few ribs.

The little man made us get back up immediately, pick up the equipment we had dropped during our fall and run to hide ourselves among nearby trees.

Dawn was breaking when we returned to base. While I was getting dressed in my gym clothes for my self-defense class, the little man who had woken me up so violently a few hours earlier came back.

"I am Bolshevik, your tactical instructor," he told me.

After joking a bit about the ordeal of the hike and the tumble we had taken jumping off the bridge, he told me that he knew about me and that he happened to be good friends with Conchita, the *compañera* of my father. At that point, the big black guy came in and Bolshevik said goodbye, promising to have breakfast with me. And after my workout, he returned in the jeep with breakfast and we had a long, intense conversation.

From that day on, Bolshevik would come by at any time, sometimes to share lunch or dinner, sometimes staying very late into the night. That's not counting those occasions when he would take us out on tactical maneuvers: retreats, ambushes and other exercises, always ending up on the bridge with the approach of the train and our inevitable leap. I discovered that the damn guy had the train's schedule down pat and did it on purpose.

Sanjurjo also visited me almost every day. He concerned himself with my progress in training, made comments about the political situation in Argentina and in Latin America generally, and told me that I could have a radio, which helped alleviate my boredom a little on the weekends.

On the last day of training, all the instructors turned out for a farewell party. There was beer and roast pork. Bolshevik and Ernesto became quite emotional, and I couldn't hide my feelings either. All the *compañeros* there were convinced of the necessity of their work. Their greatest wish was to be able to join in one of the fights that were developing around the continent. For these revolutionaries, internationalism was the highest value—an honorable duty rather than a sacrifice. As darkness approached, Román came to pick me up and take me to the Hotel Havana Libre. I felt eager to return to Argentina as a fighter, but I still had to undergo a course on "conspiratorial methods."

AFTER A FEW DAYS, I RECEIVED a phone call from Román to inform me they were ready for me to start the new course. He came by to get me in the afternoon and took me to a small apartment in the neighborhood of Vedado, very close to the Hotel Riviera. An instructor was waiting for us. His name was Fausto. He was tall and blond, with the bland face of a secret agent. First, we settled on a schedule. I had to attend from eight in the morning to five in the afternoon, Monday through Friday—the timetable of a middle-class employee. The instruction would last about five months, and was divided into three parts: conspiratorial methods, intelligence and counterinsurgency. As was the custom, we would first study theory, then move on to practice out in the streets.

The emphasis was above all on communications, verification and re-verification, and recruitment. This last topic was a source of friction between the instructor and me, or to put it more precisely, between the Cubans' preconceived methods and mine. According to them, there were three criteria for a recruitment: politics and ideology, bribery, and blackmail. I had no problem with the first. But it did not seem ethically correct to me that a revolutionary organization should buy information, and even less that it should use personal or confidential information to force someone to collaborate. Yet Fausto insisted on the protocol: study the personality of the subject you wanted to recruit, then generate compromising situations and obtain evidence, through eavesdropping or photography, that will leave him no option but to cooperate under the threat of blackmail.

They demanded a level of professionalism such as would preclude a life of normal work or study. I tried, however, to put my doubts aside and dedicate myself to learning the required techniques. I succeeded so well in making them into a lifestyle that it became hard for me to return to what I had previously held as my real self.

Intelligence was fundamentally based on the search for and analysis of information. In counterinsurgency, we studied the training manuals designed by the United States Agency for International Development (AID) for Latin American police forces. Thus we familiarized ourselves with the techniques and procedures of the enemy.

This experience played havoc with my personality. I always had a tendency to feel sorry for myself, and the training allowed me to indulge in full-blown paranoia. I saw the imperialist enemy as omniscient and omnipresent. The Americans were everywhere—they were the sea in which we Cuban fish swam.

The courses completed, I took it for granted that the Cubans would quickly arrange my departure from the island, but instead they seemed to multiply obstacles to prevent it. I naturally assumed that it had something to do with me. Later I realized that my destiny as a revolutionary was being decided by a new Cuban policy toward the Communist parties of Latin America.

After the failure of Castro's grandiose plan for a ten-million-ton sugar crop in 1970, the economic situation of the island became intractable. In 1974, a deal cut with the Soviets permitted Cubans to loosen their belts again, but it wasn't just another trade agreement—sugar for petroleum. It was much deeper—a Faustian bargain. From that point on, Cuba was required to follow the Soviet model for the management of the economy and to adhere even more scrupulously to the Soviet line in international politics. As a result, Fidel grew closer to all official Communist parties around the world, especially those in our hemisphere to which he had previously exhibited a smug superiority. In 1973, the continent had been shaken by the military coups in Chile and Uruguay. Fearful of provoking other such reactions, the pro-Soviet sector of the Cuban Communist Party turned its back on the Guevarist tradition and distanced itself from the movements committed to armed struggle, which caused friction between Cuba and the revolutionary organizations of Latin America. These abrasive relations would last until the Sandinistas' victory in Nicaragua in 1979, when a new chapter of the struggle was begun.

I should be more precise. The Cubans did not totally abandon their support for revolution in Latin America. Rather, concentrating on politics, they gave priority to relations with the Communist parties and governments of the region. At the same time, the military effort shifted from our own back yard to Africa, where the Soviets had interests for us to further in return for the help they were giving us.

Those of us revolutionaries who were in Cuba at this time found ourselves in a difficult situation as Cuban intelligence all of a sudden shortened the leash. I knew many Uruguayan Tupamaros who, after having finished military training courses, were prevented from leaving Cuba to go home and put their newly acquired knowledge into practice. Even unofficial relations among Latin American revolutionaries were discouraged by the Cubans who, on the pretext of "security concerns," tried to prevent them by every means possible. Yet we used the very same "conspiratorial methods" they had taught us to meet among ourselves in secret.

One day I was celebrating with Mónica in the Hotel Nacional. We were feeling especially happy because our first son, Jorge, had just been born. By chance and to the great annoyance of the Cubans, we bumped into the parents of Mario Roberto Santucho, the "maximum leader" of the Argentine ERP. We then made contact with the other members of the ERP who were also on the island for one reason or another, and from whom the Cubans had kept us separated. We all found that our situation was more or less the same: we were on the list for departure, but there was always some petty obstacle put in our way to keep us from leaving Cuba.

In Argentina, meanwhile, events had taken a dramatic turn that made us all feel guilty for not being there. The government of Isabel Perón had ceded control to the armed forces, whose repression was getting worse and worse. Every day the popular movement suffered new casualties. With the left almost defeated, the military staged a coup on March 24, 1976. It enjoyed the support of substantial sectors of the middle class, which demanded order and tranquility and didn't realize that in making these demands it was contributing to the opening of one of the saddest and most terrible episodes in Argentine history. The disappearances, the tortures and the murders to come would not only decimate the guerrilla movement, but brutalize anyone identified as even vaguely progressive or leftist. This state of affairs lasted until 1983.

On July 19, only four months after the coup, Mario Roberto Santucho died in combat along with other members of our organization's leadership. It was the final battle of the ERP. For us revolutionary Argentines who were in Cuba it meant a huge heartache, not only on account of the deaths of our leaders, but also because we found ourselves too far from the scene of the struggle to do anything.

"Enrique," the international representative of our now largely destroyed revolutionary organization, came to Havana. He had "run" Monica and me in Argentina. We tried to speak frankly to him about our concerns. He gave an optimistic and triumphalist analysis, but we read between the lines of his boilerplate that the situation was terrible. His own wife, a classmate of Mónica's, was among the "disappeared." The more we talked to him, the clearer it became that this was the fate of the majority of our old *compañeros*.

When we broached the subject of our return, he told us that the organization would support us but that we had to proceed cautiously in our relations with the Cubans who were now playing their own hemispheric game. He advised us to try to leave for Rome, where we would be free from the hothouse atmosphere of Havana and have greater flexibility.

When I brought up the issue of leaving, the Cubans raised a thousand obstructions and, with precise revolutionary theory, told us that for the time being, at least, the Argentine cause was lost. But I let them know that my desire to return to my country was beyond analysis, and if we really were so close to defeat or already defeated, that I believed we comrades who remained should unite to reconstruct the organization in Argentina.

As usual, the Cubans I talked to had to confer with others who were "upstairs." I waited about a week and still got no answer. I decided at that point to go straight to Piñeiro. I tried for a whole day to get an appointment with him. At three in the morning he finally called and told me to talk to his lieutenant, Morejón, who would have the answers to all my questions. But I wasn't put off so easily. I told him that if I was not allowed to leave Cuba, I would consider myself a prisoner. He told me to come to his house that morning.

At that time it was practically impossible to find public transport. A taxi, you couldn't even dream of. After an hour of walking, I arrived at Piñeiro's house. One of his assistants let me in and asked me to wait because the *comandante* was in a meeting.

As always, when Piñeiro appeared he had a smile on his face.

"What's up, Big Kid? You look so impatient!" he said in greeting.

I explained the situation and once again told him of my desire to return to my country. Stroking his beard and making expansive hand gestures à la Fidel, he made a thorough analysis of the situation in Argentina and of the ERP in particular. He concluded by explaining that he would not, out of concern for my safety, allow me to go back. They would wait for better intelligence before designing a good return plan, while in the meantime he thought our organization was in no shape to absorb returning militants.

I told Piñeiro that I would assume the risks and had already made contact with some of the ERP cadres who were in exile in Rome. To my surprise he said he had no problem with my going to Italy. We agreed on the details: I would leave soon to set up a home base; Mónica and my new son, Jorge, would follow. We would have to prepare false documentation, determine the itinerary and see about the budget. By way of saying goodbye, Piñeiro stood, asking me if I was satisfied and assuring me that we would see each other again before I left. Then his driver took me back to the hotel.

Fausto, the instructor of "conspiratorial methods," prepared the trip. In a house set up to serve as a studio, he took several photos of me for the passport and my forged Argentine identity papers. I would leave Havana by Cubana Airlines on a flight for Prague, and from there I would take a flight to Zurich, where I would catch yet another for Rome. We settled on a budget of $5,000, not including airfare. With this sum Monica and I would have to figure out how to survive by ourselves.

My farewell to Piñeiro was brief. He inquired, with his habitual precision, about all the details of the trip and, after embracing me, said, "Take care of yourself."

5
ITALY, 1976–1977

THE TRIP WENT ACCORDING TO PLAN. One of Piñeiro's men was waiting at the Prague airport to facilitate my journey to Rome. My new passport was very well made and did not arouse the slightest suspicion.

As soon as I arrived in Rome I called my contact. An Argentine with a slight Italian accent answered. He told me to go to a little café on the Piazza Venezia, where a *compañero* would come by to pick me up. I walked there with my suitcase, dazzled by the city's beauty. To me everything seemed enormous and majestic, and the women, of course, were gorgeous. I sat down on a little terrace and waited for about an hour and a half. When I was just starting to get nervous, a tall, skinny man with a large moustache came up and asked me with a thick Buenos Aires accent if I was Martín—which was, in fact, my new pseudonym. He introduced himself somewhat absurdly as "Bald Fred," and he looked more like a businessman or a con man than one of our *compañeros*. Not knowing how the party worked in Europe, I had no choice but to trust him.

Acting like a very busy executive, Bald Fred said that he couldn't attend to me at that moment and that he would register me at a hotel and come by the next day to pick me up for a talk. Without any further explanation we got into a taxi. After winding through the narrow streets of a colorful neighborhood, he dropped me off at a little hotel.

The next day, around ten in the morning, he came back and, still in a hurry, set up an appointment for that night. He told me that a *compañero* wanted to meet me and I should be punctual. What struck me the most was that the encounter would take place on a street corner and not at a bar or restaurant. It seemed wholly unnecessary to take such extreme security measures in a place like Rome.

At 9 P.M., after having spent a day touring that wonderful city, I went to the meeting place. I studied the route ahead of time in order to gauge the exact moment of my passing by that corner. I was almost there when the *compañero* I was supposed to meet intercepted me. There was no need for introductions: he was Pelado Gorriarán, who at that time was one of the best known and most prestigious leaders of the ERP. He was an almost mythic figure who had directed or participated in our principal military operations. Seeing him, I immediately understood why they had taken so many security precautions. Pelado was one of the Argentine security forces' Ten Most Wanted.

We ate in a quiet neighborhood trattoria. Pelado asked me with great interest about the situation in Cuba, and he seemed surprised when I told him of my difficulties leaving the island. He had a sober view of our situation in Argentina. Although he could not accept that we were defeated, he conceded the extent of our weakness. Then, with the optimism that was as much a part of us as our Marxism, he said he believed that if we remained tenacious, we could change everything.

With regard to my return to Argentina, he said I would have to wait until the leadership had more detailed reports from home before being able to plan the return of the large group of *compañeros* who were then in Europe. Meanwhile, I would take part in the solidarity front's efforts in Italy. Under Gorriarán's direction, I was also to help out with assignments aimed at strengthening the party apparatus, finding more financial resources, and supporting logistical activities connected to our military operations inside Argentina. For the time being, I was supposed to remain in Italy. Gorriarán said that when he needed me, he would contact me.

Italy itself seemed to be on the brink. A year earlier, in 1976, the Communist Party, hard on the heels of the ruling Christian Democrats, had obtained its best electoral results ever. The labor movement was combative. The extreme left had thousands of militants and published several daily papers. The Red Brigades were causing chaos with a terror campaign that culminated in the kidnapping and murder of Aldo Moro.

But the only war we cared about was five thousand miles away. In 1977, the Argentinean "disappeared" numbered in the thousands. We did not consider ourselves refugees, but soldiers in transit, awaiting the call to arms. So as not to compromise our sanctuary, we did not want to meddle too much in Italian internal affairs.

I contacted "Manuel the Basque," the man in charge of the ERP in Italy. He told me that I had to settle in Milan, where a group of *compañeros* connected to us, but not actually members of the party, lived. Milan was attractive because it was where the Italian labor movement was strongest. I would have to concentrate on solidarity work there and in Genoa and Turin, where we also had *compañeros*.

We argued for a long time over the party's position with respect to solidarity. It had to be broad and with a democratic character to mobilize the largest number of Italians in support of the Argentine struggle: from the Christian Democrats to the ultra-left. The ERP would maintain relations and exchange political information with any Latin American revolutionary organizations that had a presence in the cities where we operated, as well as with the other Argentine groups. Clandestine activities that might come up would be totally independent of the solidarity work; we would avoid carrying out such operations in countries where we had a support base and maintained political relations.

Our main effort focused on the Italian labor unions. At first, it was not easy. Many didn't even want to listen to us. The Argentine Communist Party was giving "critical support" to the dictatorship in Buenos Aires and had better international relations than we did. We decided to bypass the labor bureaucrats and work directly with the internal committees of the factories.

We had some successes. The workers of Carlo Herba and Farmitalia, for instance, donated a day of their salaries each month to help Argentine political prisoners. The Genovese stevedores secretly loaded thousands of handbills expressing solidarity with the Argentine working class and opposition to the dictatorship onto each ship that left for our country. Many young Italians without political affiliation dedicated their efforts to solidarity with our people, and more than one put his life at risk by personally delivering a clandestine message to Argentina. The factory-level workers' committees demanded that their national unions issue statements against the dictatorship in our country. We spoke to their assemblies and shared our lives with them. Many *compañeros* who had been obliged to flee Argentina found refuge and solidarity in the homes of Italian workers.

Meanwhile, Monica and my son, Jorge, arrived. I had not been living at a permanent address. Being alone, I had stayed wherever someone put out a mattress for me when night fell. With a two-year-old son, such improvisation was no longer feasible. That's how we got to know Vito and Lucía—he a worker at Fiat, she a student. They lived in a small apartment in a working-class neighborhood with their son, Camu, who was the same age as my boy. They had only one room, a tiny living space—but unlimited generosity. At their invitation, we moved in.

ONE DAY I RECEIVED AN URGENT CALL asking me to travel to Rome. When I arrived, Manuel the Basque was waiting for me in the Termini Roma train station with another *compañero* I didn't recognize. I was surprised by this man's height and his flaming red hair. I learned that he was "Skinny" Santiago, a legend in the organization. He had been chief of a mountain company of guerrillas in the province of Tucumán and had become famous for his valor in combat. He had taken part in the ERP's most important actions.

Unlike our other military chieftains, Santiago exuded charisma and aroused sympathy. He had a joke or a smile for everyone. His common-law wife was detained in Argentina along with his four-year-old son, whom he had been able to see only twice in his life. He talked about him all the time.

We entered a café. Skinny got right to the heart of the matter: a group of *compañeros* was preparing to go fight in Namibia alongside the SWAPO guerrillas, and they thought I might want to go. Skinny would be the leader. I told him I didn't know anything about Namibia, but I would be happy to have the chance to see combat, and honored to go at his side. The plan was to travel to Angola and, after completing a commando course there, infiltrate into Namibia.

We got together in an apartment in Rome that the SWAPO people had loaned us, and waited almost two months. In the end, everything fell apart when the group in Angola that we were supposed to work with attempted a premature coup. They were all executed by firing squad.

Subsequently I was ordered to Spain to link up with Gorriarán, who had already gone there from Rome. This sounded even better than Africa because I thought surely it had to do with some activity related to Argentina, possibly with my return there.

We met in Barcelona. As always, we paid a lot of attention to security precautions in our meetings. I met Pelado on a corner and he didn't even say hello. He told me under his breath to follow him some six blocks through the Gothic quarter, while another *compañero* walked behind us to make sure no one was following.

He entered an old bar and I followed. The other *compañero* also joined us and sat down at our table. After asking me about the situation in Italy and the solidarity work I had been doing with labor organizations, he informed me that the party's long-range plans could not be carried out for lack of funds. Therefore we would have to finance ourselves by European operations—which meant kidnappings.

I was not surprised. I knew the difficult position we were in, and at several meetings with the leadership I had already proposed the identical solution. The only concern I had was that, in case I was arrested, the solidarity work and the contacts I had made up to now would be compromised. He responded that I shouldn't worry, that all who participated in such activities would leave a signed letter of resignation from the party; if we were arrested, we would be disowned and would have to claim in our public statements that we were common criminals.

I was against kidnapping noncombatants if the motive was solely economic, no matter how urgent. It seemed to me a form of cruelty that was incompatible with the ideals that supposedly inspired us. It is true, however, that the hundreds of thousands of dollars collected in Europe through these means allowed us to smuggle out of Argentina many clandestine *compañeros* whose lives were in danger. In fact, the safety of those who had gone underground inside the country was increasingly questionable. In April 1977, in a meeting of the party executive committee, a plan was adopted which called for spiriting "burned ones" out of the country, organizing political schools in exile, and preparing a plan for the massive return of cadres to form a military nucleus in the mountains.

The kidnappings financed all this. I understood their necessity, but I was glad when instead of being given a gun and a mask, I was ordered to return to Italy and "work with the masses."

WE ORGANIZED FIVE SCHOOLS for theoretical training in three basic fields, with thirty participants in each course: political, military, trade union. They were established in different regions and the courses lasted six months. Ours took place in a little farm town near Brescia, where we presented ourselves openly as militants of the Argentine resistance. Our neighbors gave us food and lodging. For our part, we helped out with some community work. It was a strange encounter between two worlds.

In our schools, we continued to wage our long-distance war by perpetuating its rituals. The day began with a military drill in the center of the patio and a salute to the flag of the ERP. We were obsessed with our dead and disappeared, animated by the will never to surrender.

The formal study of texts entailed reflection and discussion, which naturally resulted in political arguments, especially over the question of armed struggle. Without saying so openly, the faction led by the ERP general secretary of that time, Luis Martini—probably under the influence of the Communist Party—wanted to abandon it. Another current of opinion, clearly martial in character and identified with Gorriarán, urged a return to Argentina to fight. The latter faction favored the establishment of a core guerrilla cadre in the mountains, followed by infiltration into the cities of operational teams linked to the trade union movement. The party would not reveal itself as such, so as not to provoke a violent military reaction. A general assessment of previous failures was reduced down to technical considerations: fundamental rules of guerrilla warfare had been violated and a temporary setback or two should not cause anyone to question the overall Marxist-Leninist strategy of armed struggle.

I was on the side of the maximalists. Our leader, Gorriarán, was now in Colombia with the FARC guerrillas, and had been replaced by Santiago, who followed the same hard line. In the middle of this imbroglio, we were visited by a member of the political bureau who accused us of "militaristic deviation." Santiago was subsequently and without delay exiled to Spain. To browbeat me into full acceptance of correct principles of Marxist theory, I was asked to join a group of comrades from Sweden. I had an affair with the wife of one of them, which I felt obliged to report to the leadership. When a member of the central directorate arrived, he raised the issue of "moral problems"—asking me to explain my situation. Furious, I responded that I would not discuss my personal life in public. After this heartfelt outburst, I considered the issue behind me.

Soon after, Gorriarán finally returned from Colombia and laid out a realistic plan to inject an armed group of commandos into the mountains of Argentina. I wanted to be part of it, of course. But then he informed me that the political bureau opposed my participation "for moral reasons." He personally did not ascribe much significance to the matter, but I had to settle things. I decided to ask the Swedish woman to go back to Sweden and I promised I would soon follow her. It was a bad lie, the end of an affair—and the formal and bitter resolution of the "moral problem."

THE FACTIONALISM GREW IN INTENSITY and became homicidal. I returned to Milan, back to the home of Vito and Lucía, where Mónica and

Jorge were waiting for me. Gorriarán moved to Paris. Every time I contacted him to ask when we could take up arms, he advised me to be patient. Meanwhile, I continued carrying out "solidarity activities," until one day I got a call from Gorriarán's wife in Paris, advising me to come immediately. When I arrived, Gorriarán informed me that the political bureau considered one of our members, Daniel Martín, an "enemy agent." They had asked Gorriarán to "put him to the test." When he refused, the political bureau issued a "Bulletin 113," publicly accusing Daniel Martín of being an enemy agent and accusing Gorriarán of having protected him. One of the leaders went so far as to declare that thirteen comrades, of whom I was one, should be condemned to death for counterrevolutionary activity. On our side, some comrades even considered the possibility of seizing the initiative by liquidating the secretary-general—and then blaming it on the Argentine secret service. Fortunately the majority, including Gorriarán, was opposed to such a fratricidal act.

Such were the extremism and intrigues of a closed, sectarian group that lived on its ghosts, poisoned by an exile that prevented us from seeing how absurd our internecine struggle was. We had convinced ourselves that we were at "at war," and that during war, treason—from whatever source—must be punished. What we didn't see was that our war was largely a war of words, and that in such a conflict one always runs the risk of being accused of treason by anyone at all. Subsequently, we would learn that the accusations against Gorriarán had clearly been manufactured by members of Cuban intelligence. When I brought it up with them later in Nicaragua in 1979, they justified themselves by saying they had been fed disinformation by one of their agents, a member of the Argentine Communist Party who later turned out to be a double agent working for the Argentine army intelligence.

Certainly the ERP was now split in half. Toward the end of 1978 we tried to heal the wound by organizing a general meeting in Paris, but the members of the Central Committee could not leave Cuba, where they were practically held under house arrest because Cuba was still supporting the Argentine Communist Party as part of its new obedience to Moscow's "conservative" line. We decided to go forward anyhow; we would return to Argentina to set up an armed insurgency in the northern jungle. We would need quite a bit of money, so we decided to organize a team in Spain, where we had a base of support and where the Argentine secret service at that time moved less freely even than in France.

The first priority was to obtain arms for self-protection and then move on to money-raising operations. I managed to acquire two revolvers, which I took to Spain, where Gorriarán and Martín were based. We engaged in several bank robberies, although one of them resulted in three of our people being arrested. Two of the *compañeros* stuck to the story that it was just a common crime. But the third stupidly defended himself by insisting that he was a militant of the Argentine resistance. All three were jailed.

I was sent back to Italy once again. Returning to Argentina had become difficult and our stay in Europe was going nowhere. Soon we would have to look reality in the face: to become involved in a crucial way, or accept the fact that we'd have to leave revolution behind and start a new life in Europe.

Fortunately, there was a new development in Nicaragua that offered an out. As the Sandinistas began to make real gains, I decided to resolve my dilemma by leaving the party and its internal squabbles to fight for the guerrillas.

It was not an auspicious moment. A few weeks earlier, the first attempt at an insurrection against the Somoza regime had been put down by the Nicaraguan military. Yet I sensed that going to Central America represented an exit toward daylight. Maybe our frustrated hopes would be reborn in Nicaragua.

Once again I went to Paris to let Gorriarán know what I had decided. He approved, especially because we had very good relations with the Sandinista Front, and they needed a new group of comrades with training like ours. The decision to send several of us to Nicaragua was ratified at a formal meeting of our group.

The paperwork for obtaining Panamanian visas was already under way. As for the plane tickets, I felt it would have been indecent to ask the impoverished Sandinistas for them. We approached a group of sympathetic left-wing Christians in Paris and they bought our tickets for us.

6

Panama–Costa Rica, 1979

FTER GETTING TO PANAMA WE PLANNED to contact the Sandinistas so they could infiltrate us into Nicaragua. I felt buoyant. I was leaving behind me the internal fights of the party and the discontents of exile. Yet I was also leaving Italy, with its sympathetic people, my children and their mother, and friends who would never let me down.

The flight was long and difficult. At a stopover in Madrid, the plane was delayed for twenty-four hours. Given my pent-up desire for action, the delay was unbearable. Surely my Argentine comrades were already in Panama. What would they think of me if I didn't show up? And what if they left without me? Even worse, what if my late arrival threw off the Sandinista contact and everything fell apart because of me? Those were my worries.

Havana was the last stopover. It felt strange to be there as a foreigner, with a passport in my pocket in the name of "Ignacio Molina," my latest fictional incarnation. To be there only in transit, without having a chance to embrace my sister or see my friends, was bizarre and dreamlike. But the *compañeros* were waiting.

It was my first time in Panama. Even though my passport was poorly made, I passed through immigration without any problem. Since my only luggage was a small carryon item, I didn't even have to wait in the baggage line. It was the way I would travel in the years to come. For the undercover agent, believe it or not, baggage claim is more risky than passport control. That is where informers concentrate—the place where they have the most time to snoop.

After leaving the airport, my taxi exited at a giant shopping center that seemed to go on forever, marked with the stamp of gringo bad taste. The only thing I liked was the brightly painted buses, with their radios turned up full blast, playing salsa and merengue. They made you feel like dancing in the middle of the street. The taxi left me at the Hotel Roma, which at that time was small and cheap but comfortable. The heat was intense. After dropping off my bag, I went out into the street, acting like a carefree tourist. I called my contact.

"Hello, is that Boris? This is your nephew from San José. Can we meet?" I spoke according to script.

"Sure, man. I was waiting for you. I'll be right there," a voice with a strong Nicaraguan accent answered.

I felt relaxed. I took a taxi to the McDonald's on Via España, where the Nicaraguan and I had agreed to meet in an hour. It was still early, so I took a stroll around the neighborhood. At McDonald's once again, I placed the magazine *Cambio 16* on my table, with a pack of Gitanes cigarettes on top.

Boris arrived on schedule. Looking at tables and not faces, he saw the magazine and pack of cigarettes and came over to greet me. He was in his thirties but looked young—too young to be my uncle.

Speaking quietly, I asked about the other *compañeros*. He said they had left for Nicaragua the previous day. He told me not to worry. If there was no flight the next day, he would send me by land, and although it was very difficult to get a visa for Costa Rica, they had a good clandestine conveyor belt across the border. Then we talked for a long time about the war the Sandinistas were waging.

"This time we're really going to win," he said. "The *compitas* are fighting for victory or death, and if the gringos get involved, we'll thrash them too."

We met again the following morning. There was no flight, so that afternoon I had to take a bus to Davíd, a town near the Costa Rican border. Boris said his son would continue with me as far as San José.

I was fortunate that I had almost no luggage, because the bus was full of sacks and chickens. The majority of the passengers were peasants who went to Panama City to buy or sell something and they returned heavily laden. Others were smalltime smugglers, carrying all kinds of cheap merchandise purchased in the Colón Free Zone to resell on the other side to others who were smugglers or would-be smugglers attempting to sneak across the border.

Boris's son was thirteen or fourteen years old. Despite his youth, he carried out the assignments entrusted to him with great seriousness. But he didn't like to talk, and this made the journey interminable.

We arrived at Davíd at night, walked a few blocks and knocked on the door of a humble little house. An elderly man, half asleep and obviously a peasant, opened the door and invited us in.

"What's up, *compas?* Wait. I'll get you something to eat."

That was all he said.

After a while he came back with two plates of steaming soup, meat and boiled plantains. After we ate, while we were drinking coffee, Boris's son explained to him that we had to cross the border. "Like the *compas* I brought last week," he added.

Without saying anything, the old man lit a cigarette and went outside. I settled in as best I could in an old armchair and, looking at one of the many enormous spider webs stretched across the ceiling, fell asleep.

It was not yet dawn when they woke me. We got into a truck, which the old man drove, shouting at it to get moving as if it were a horse. Thus we crossed the Costa Rican border at Paso Canoas. We encountered just one border post, where, to my surprise, the guards saluted the old man from a distance. He didn't even respond to their greeting.

Dawn was breaking when we entered a small village. "From this point on there are no more border posts," said the old man as he put on the brakes.

When I got out of the truck I went over to him to say goodbye. He responded with a powerful handshake. *"Patria libre!"* he said, showing his tobacco-stained teeth when he smiled.

Then there was another bus with sacks and chickens. Staggering and with an aching back, I arrived in San José, Costa Rica's capital. Boris's son made some phone calls and told me we would meet the *compañeros* in Central Park, close to the bus station. We walked over, and waited for them to come by to pick me up. After a simple introduction—"This is the *compa*"—Boris's son embraced me and left.

They took me in a Japanese pickup truck to a house on the outskirts of the city where there were about twenty guerrillas. Some were waiting to go into Nicaragua; others had been there already and had been wounded, and now were recuperating in order to fight again. After about two hours, during which I asked a thousand questions and heard a thousand fantastic war stories, the person in charge of the house arrived and told me that we would be leaving for the front next morning. He advised me to take this opportunity to rest.

That night I had trouble sleeping. It was a relief for me to be summoned to breakfast. I couldn't wait to get going so I would meet up with my comrades and with "Comrade FAL," as they called the rifle that was the guerrillas' weapon of choice.

At last, aboard a little bus, we set out on the road. There were eight or nine of us. The Costa Rican guards waved at us as we went by.

"Good luck, *compas!*" they called out.

"Patria libre!" we answered.

We arrived in Liberia, very close to the border. Throughout the area, Sandinista fighters were coming and going. We went to a house where we were supposed to hand over the documents and foreign currency we were carrying; I turned in the money, but hid my passport. We also had to fill out some cards with our legal names, aliases, nationality and—this sent a small chill down my spine—the name of someone to notify in case of death.

They distributed a weapon to each of us, a FAL rifle with four clips of ammunition. After forming ranks, we began the march to the border. I was finally going into battle.

WE TREKKED AT NIGHT under an immense moon. Fortunately, the terrain was not difficult and we advanced rapidly. As the realization that we were in Nicaragua began to sink in, I felt an intense emotion. At the same time, I was aware of being in totally unfamiliar territory. If I got lost, I would be in a desperate situation; I concentrated all of my attention on the man marching in front of me, and the full moon was my best companion at that moment.

We made a rest stop before continuing at dawn. This permitted us to pair off in comradely fashion and disperse around the area. That's how I got to know Jotana, my first Nicaraguan *compañero*. He was from the rural area of Rivas and about my age, twenty-three, but already a seasoned guerrilla. He told me that a few months earlier Somoza's National Guard had arrived at his village with the intention of forcing him to join up. With two friends, he decided to escape and left for Costa Rica. In San José he had done a little of everything: shoeshine boy, waiter, mason's helper. Many young Nicaraguans had had similar experiences. "Sometimes they didn't even pay us," he said. "They just gave us food and a place to sleep."

That was why he made contact with the Sandinistas; he wanted to liberate his country, see his mother again, and work on his farm where he'd had his own horse.

I asked him about the two friends from his village. For the first time his expression became somber. "They died in the capture of Peñas Blancas three days ago," he answered with downcast eyes.

Dawn came while we were talking. I saw that we were surrounded by very green hills. To the right, I could make out an immense lake that seemed to have no limits. Distracted by the beauty of our surroundings, I barely heard the order to form ranks. Jotana moved ahead, putting the agreed-upon five feet between us. We began marching again. By now there were forty or so men in our column.

The heat pressed down on me; the leather bag with my coat and ammunition grew heavier; the rifle strap chafed my neck; my mood fell precipitously.

I don't remember if it was the first loud explosion or the sight of Jotana running away that caused me to react, but instinctively I took off running behind him. Suddenly it was raining mortar rounds everywhere, each whistling down in that eerie way that seems to say that it's going to fall right on your head. At one point I saw a small bush and struggled to take cover underneath, though I knew that if the shell were to land there, the bush would be blown away. Luckily, I spotted Jotana, who was signaling me.

"Let's get into the ditch," he shouted. "One has already fallen in, so it's impossible that another will."

I ignored the illogicality and threw myself face down into the dry creek bed that Jotana was pointing to. I tried to remember all the guerrilla tactics that Bolshevik had taught me during the military training courses in Cuba. But all I could manage was decidedly uncommunist: Pray to all the saints.

If I managed to preserve my dignity throughout the bombardment, it was because there was no Swedish consulate to go to for asylum. Urban operations and clandestine work, difficult and dangerous though they are, were a completely different proposition from this war the Sandinistas were fighting. As the shells continued to fall, you could hear explosions and shouts everywhere. Mud and rock rained down on our bodies.

After a while, the explosions became more infrequent until they ceased completely. We had taken a large number of casualties. We carried them with us as we renewed the march in much smaller groups and at a much more accelerated pace. At this point I was incapable of taking any initiative, and clung to Jotana like a life preserver.

Even though the mortar attack had ceased, the soldiers were worried. I asked Jotana what was wrong. He explained that surely Somoza's Air Force would be coming soon because the planes always followed the mortars.

Twenty minutes later, we heard the sound of engines above us. The airplanes dropped 500-pound bombs and strafed us with their

.50-caliber machine guns. We were ordered to shoot at the planes, but they flew too high and too fast for our FAL rifles. Even so, just firing at them made me feel better.

When the planes had left, one of the fighters came up to me and said, "You have to get used to it, *compa*. Those sons of bitches come every single morning."

The truth is I never got used to it, and every time I heard those planes I felt a pang of fear.

I have no idea how we wound up near the same point where we had commenced the march. Many of us had been killed and many wounded. I felt happy because I hadn't been hit. But this emotion plunged me into revolutionary guilt.

THE WAR WAS ABSURDLY MONOTONOUS. The Air Force in the morning, the interminable marches, the perpetual ambushes. Trenches dug where we passed the days and nights. Small victories and defeats.

I don't know how much time had passed when by chance I met with Pelado Gorriarán. The encounter was joyful. I told him about my journey to Nicaragua and he was surprised that I had had to make it alone; I explained that other *compañeros* were supposed to have traveled with me but they decided not to at the last minute, claiming family problems. We agreed that such excuses were the moral equivalent of desertion. Yet in fact they were people who had spent years underground, including years in prison or exile in Europe. And we were in no position to understand or judge them: the idea that one might decide to give priority to loved ones was simply not part of our vocabulary.

Pelado's presence was important to me not only because of the affection I had for him but because of what he represented as a symbol of continuity in the long Argentinean struggle. It was morning when we met and this meant the usual air attack. But we were so happy to see each other that we paid scant attention to Somoza's planes and kept on talking as though still calmly seated at a sidewalk café in Rome.

Pelado said that everything we were learning in Nicaragua could be taken home to Argentina later on, and that our presence in the battle zone would raise the morale of our comrades who had stayed behind in Europe. Hearing about our sacrifice, they would embrace the Argentine liberation movement more enthusiastically.

We were hardly the only foreigners among the Sandinistas who shared those dreams. Colombians, Chileans, Peruvians, Mexicans,

Salvadorans—it was the Latin American equivalent of an international brigade. The conservative press, in Nicaragua and elsewhere, was labeling those who went to fight as mercenaries, but I know that I wasn't paid. We fought because Somoza represented everything we hated and because those who supported him were the very same who sustained dictatorships in our own countries.

There were some funny moments to go along with the chest-thumping. On one occasion, for instance, I found myself alongside a Chilean with whom I had gone through the Cuban military schools. He was shouting into his walkie-talkie: "Stop speaking nonsense! Tell me how many they are! That's fine but goddamnit tell me how many!" He kept repeating these words with desperate urgency.

I asked him what was going on, and he told me that Somoza's National Guard had taken a nearby hill and we had sent a scout squad to find out how many troops were there so we could prepare a counterattack. They already had the enemy under observation, but, when he asked for the number of National Guardsmen, the only answer that came through the radio was: "A whole lot, *compa!* You wouldn't believe how many, man!"

The contrast between the Chilean, who had formal academic military training, and the Nicaraguans, who had learned from actual guerrilla fighting, as well as the absurd dialogue over the walkie-talkie struck me as highly comical. Of course I also understood the Chilean's frustration.

On another occasion, we heard that some helicopters carrying North American troops had landed on Costa Rican territory. We thought surely this meant Yankee intervention. With the Americans behind us and Somoza's crack troops under the notorious Major Bravo's command in front of us, the consequences would surely prove disastrous. But the Sandinistas showed a battle élan that eventually inspired all of us.

"Now we'll take the measure of those gringo sons of bitches," they were saying among themselves. But the U.S. intervention turned out to be just another war rumor.

The Nicaraguan Air Force planes kept coming with their murderous payloads of napalm and 500-pound bombs, but we finally received delivery of four Cuban anti-aircraft guns the Costa Ricans had held onto for several weeks.

We heard them firing their first shots. They didn't score a hit, but they caused the pilot to climb higher and return to base. It was the last airplane I saw in the war.

A few days later Somoza resigned and fled the country, just as Batista had fled Cuba twenty years earlier. The Sandinista troops from the northern and southern fronts closed in on Managua.

7

MANAGUA, JULY 1979

JULY 19, 1979, WAS THE DAY THE REVOLUTION triumphed. In Managua, people were firing their guns at the sky. It was a moment of jubilation and festivity. The People's Revolutionary Army of Argentina was represented. We felt that our dead and disappeared were there also and were celebrating the victory with us.

There were six of us when we left Europe. At that time we hadn't even known exactly where Nicaragua was. But we knew that it was the site of a revolutionary war we talked so much about and couldn't pull off in our own country. The victory took away the bitter taste of defeat that had been with us so long.

We Argentines had become separated during the course of the war. We reunited on July 20, the day after the fall of Somoza. We all met in Managua. We were amazed: none of us had been killed or even wounded. We were just tired, with the sleepless faces that only war can sculpt. We each had something extraordinary to tell. We embraced. We loved each other.

Skinny Santiago was with us, with his beard and fiery red hair, tall and thin as a beanpole. Pelado Gorriarán was too, his bald head sunburned, his beard bleached, and his bug eyes making him seem even more surprised than usual. Manuel the Basque, with his sleepy face and his perpetual headaches. "The Cat," with the pallor of a recent university graduate and his inexhaustible vitality. "Fat Man" Sanchez, who had lost a few pounds, but whose good sense of humor had not been diminished by the war.

All of us were armed. All of us dressed in olive drab—the six-man Argentine legion of the ERP.

Santiago and The Cat had been in the artillery; Pelado in the general staff; the Basque in logistics; Fat Man Sanchez in troop transport.

57

I had fought on the front line and at the end in a commando squad.

The first two went back to their unit, now part of the new People's Sandinista Army. The Fat Man went to work organizing the Sandinista militias. The remaining three of us decided to put ourselves at the disposition of the Sandinistas for whatever they deemed necessary. But in the euphoric disorder of the Revolution, we didn't know whom to approach. Since we had nowhere to sleep that night, we found a space in what had been Somoza's old bunker. After eating some canned food we found there, we sat down to confer. We were joined by a mulatto who extracted a bottle of rum from his backpack and offered it to us; we accepted with relish.

We could immediately tell by his accent that he was a Cuban, but we didn't let on. Pelado had already spotted him during the war in the high command of the Sandinista Front, accompanied by other Cubans. As we tossed down a second round, he told us, almost as a confession, what his nationality was, that his name was Pino, and that he was a communications specialist. Discretion, as I was aware, is not the Cubans' strong point.

We took the opportunity to explain our situation to him and ask if he could tell us where to go so that someone could make use of our services. He promised to speak with his superior officer and we agreed to meet again the next day in the officers' mess. We continued drinking and chatting about our families, the war, our countries, and everything one talks about in such circumstances, especially under the influence of rum.

The next day, despite our hangovers, we rose at dawn. We were all happy because now we had a contact and could foresee fresh possibilities in the long process of consolidating the victory we had won.

We agreed that Pelado would go first, because he was our chief. The Basque and I would wait for him in the Intercontinental Hotel.

Armed and uniformed men were coming and going from the hotel along with television crews from all over the world. In surroundings of such luxury, it was surrealistic to see fighters lounging around as they pleased, without letting go of their rifles, and others running about in all directions as if they were on maneuvers. By midday, Pelado had still not come back. At about two in the afternoon, he finally showed up; one look at his smiling face told us things had gone well.

He had met with the Cubans who were organizing state security for Daniel Ortega; they felt that our clandestine experience in Argentina and Europe would prove useful at the least. Santiago and the Cat could remain in artillery and Fat Man Sanchez in the militia. Pelado asked me to come with him. I was to return to meet the Cubans, two of whom said they knew me.

I immediately recognized Alejandro and Renán. I had met the former in Havana, where he worked with Piñeiro in the Americas Department. The latter was in charge of the special military schools during the time I had taken my courses in Cuba. There were two others, Tony de la Guardia and a man called "Bear." I had not known them in Cuba, but I had crossed paths with them during the war, on the southern front, shortly after my arrival in Nicaragua. One day I had been in the rearguard looking for ammunition for our grenade launcher; not finding any in the armory, I ended up asking someone, who advised me to speak with "the Spaniards." This moniker surprised me: I knew there were combatants from all over the world, but I could not imagine there'd be anyone from Spain.

Someone pointed out where the famous Spaniards were. I went to meet them and was stunned to hear unmistakable Cuban accents. Now I recognized Tony and Bear as those "Spaniards" I had met on the southern front. Tony, of course, was something of a legend, having served as logistics honcho for the Sandinistas, arranging weapons deliveries from Cuba via Panama and taking part in combat.

The next day we got to work. We had to do a little bit of everything: look for a typewriter, carry out the arrest of an ex–National Guardsman, track down snipers who were still prowling the outskirts of Managua, and even conduct interrogations. Now and then we would lie down to sleep wherever we happened to be.

There was about a month of these different activities, then a permanent assignment. Renán Montero, a Cuban I had met in the military school, had just been named chief of the Sandinista intelligence service and he wanted me in his group. He had a long history of involvement in Nicaragua, having joined the famous Carlos Fonseca in the first attempt to overthrow Somoza in 1959, and having later served under my father in the doomed venture in the Argentinean mountains.

I had no experience in this new role, although the courses in Cuba and my participation in urban operations involving robbery, assault and kidnapping helped me face my new mission.

One day I went to see Pelado Gorriarán, who had remained in state security. He told me that thanks to some intelligence from a woman they had detained, it might be possible to find Major Bravo, the infamous chief of operations of the National Guard, well known for his assassinations and his cruelty toward prisoners of war. Liquidation of this man would be a great blow to the counterrevolution. Since he was living abroad, the operation was under my service's control.

Pelado's intelligence reports were really first class since they came from Bravo's own mistress, who had then, in turn, started an amorous relationship with Pelado himself. The woman did not act out of sympathy with the Sandinistas, but because she had received, in exchange for her services, a mansion in the town of León for herself and her mother. We immediately began to put together a plan of execution. Thanks to the informant's collaboration, the assignment seemed straightforward, but with an element of risk.

We decided that the participants should be foreigners, because in case of failure, casualties or arrests, the Sandinistas, who were now forming a government, would not then be implicated. With this consideration in mind, the other Argentine *compañeros* were brought into the service. They installed us in a villa and fabricated six sets of false documents.

Meanwhile, we continued to develop our plan. It seemed possible to draw Bravo into a "honey trap." Not suspecting betrayal, he had contacted his mistress, inviting her to meet him in Honduras in a house in Tegucigalpa where he had taken refuge. At the last minute we decided that only two would go on the operation: Pelado and one other. I was excluded because the other operative was more experienced and because if I was captured, my name ("son of Masetti") would implicate Cuba. Frustrated, I could do nothing else but dedicate myself to the logistical and communications aspects of the operation.

One afternoon, a short time after the departure of my two comrades, I was in Renán's office. Julia, his secretary, called us out so we could hear the news on Honduran radio. Bravo had been found dead, shot in the head at a house on the outskirts of Tegucigalpa. No one had been arrested and everything seemed to indicate that it was a settling of scores among former Somoza military men, the announcer said. Bravo, totally unsuspecting, had arrived without a bodyguard at the house where his inamorata was waiting. But Pelado was also there with his pistol and killed him.

The operation was a total success. Not only had the objective been attained, but there was no indication that the executioners were Argentine revolutionaries linked to the Sandinistas.

Not everything went so smoothly. Even before Pelado had left Honduras, other Argentine comrades began to arrive in Nicaragua. And once again there was a difference of opinion about how to rebuild the party in Argentina. Occasionally, the political debate threatened to turn into actual fighting. The poisonous atmosphere caused Manuel the Basque and me and a small group of comrades to distance ourselves from the whole affair. We quit the party without the slightest intention of constituting a faction or of committing ourselves to an alternative approach. Everyone would search for and choose his own way.

It was a very painful decision. The party was my family. Ever since we had met, I had felt close to Pelado, but I felt that he had instituted a "cult of personality," destroying the notion of collective leadership and centralizing power in his hands.

To be sure, the Sandinista victory had rekindled our spirit. The victory, though, was not portable, especially inasmuch as we were preparing to intervene in a country—*our* country—that after so many years in exile we no longer understood. The upshot was that we were attempting to return to Argentina with already-failed ideas and proposals, to transplant the Nicaraguan experience without acknowledging how different the situations were.

NICARAGUAN INTELLIGENCE—WHICH IS TO SAY Cuban intelligence, which was clearly in control—had decided to follow the assassination of Comandante Bravo with an even grander target: Somoza himself. But during the planning of this mission, the political arguments among my Argentine *compañeros* became so acrimonious that I finally couldn't stand it any more and asked to be discharged.

Once again I found myself without a precise task. I presented myself at the Office of Personnel and Cadre of the Sandinista Army to ask for an assignment. I was ordered to go to the fifth military region in the southeastern area of Nicaragua, whose headquarters was in Chontales. Upon arrival, I discovered that the region commander was "Major Emilio"—Javier Pichardo, chief of operations on the southern front during the war.

Emilio suggested that I join the operations staff of the regional border guards. When I explained to him that I knew nothing about such work, he laughed and told me that everyone was learning and anyhow I shouldn't worry because periodically they would give training seminars to each unit.

And so I arrived in San Carlos, the departmental capital of Rio San Juan on the Costa Rican border, where the border guards of that region were based.

My work consisted in setting up posts along the entire length of the frontier, and in the training and management of the mobile squad that would be based in San Carlos—preparing them for combat in the event of the expected Yankee penetration—as well as the carrying out of other preventive measures.

The rank and file lived in the old barracks of the National Guard. We officers had a house, a state of affairs that only served to emphasize unfair differences between us and the troops, whose circumstances did not meet even minimal sanitary conditions.

One day, when I was talking with the sector chief, I learned that there was a large ranch nearby that had been donated to the Sandinista Front by the poet Coronel Hurtecho. It was unoccupied. We went to inspect the place and saw that it really would be an ideal location for our people. In addition to pleasant surroundings, the geography was perfect for organizing the defense and general protection of the town.

We began investigating and found that the ranch had already been assigned to the brand new Nicaraguan Institute for Agrarian Reform. We immediately requested an interview with the area head of that agency. After passing through four secretaries and seven bodyguards, we managed to get to the office of the person in question, whose real name I cannot recall—though I do remember that he was called *"Raspacoco"*—roughly, "Coconut Shredder." As soon as I saw him, I understood why: his teeth were so enormous that they gave his whole face an unusual and ridiculous look. He received us wearing heavy cologne and a pearly white *guayabera*.

We had not even finished making our recommendation when this fellow became hysterical. He immediately accused us of arrogance and of trying to appropriate everything. With the air conditioning on full blast while our men sweltered outside, he shouted, "And if the National Guard used to live in those barracks why shouldn't your soldiers be able to live there too?"

I wore myself out trying to explain to him that Sandinista *compañeros* could not be compared to Somoza's Guard, that we were supposed to be building a better world, and that objectively the barracks were falling apart. Left with no arguments, but with the same bad temper, Raspacoco finally told us in a conspiratorial tone: "Actually, I can't turn the ranch over to you because it is a protocol house of the National Directorate."

We gave up arguing, but I decided to do a little investigating on my own to discover the reason for this functionary's stubbornness.

After interviewing the watchmen at the house, and some neighbors, I learned that "Coconut Shredder" was using the place for his own parties. Along with an outline of our needs and the way the ranch was being used for decadent bourgeois pleasures, I sent a report to Major Pichardo, who answered immediately by giving us his full support and an order allowing us to take the place over. Unfortunately we couldn't do it because at that very moment, Comandante Jaime Wheelock, a member of the Sandinista National Directorate and the man in charge of agrarian reform, visited San Carlos and blocked the operation.

The *compañeros* continued living in lamentable conditions, but now the Directorate had a protocol/pleasure house in San Carlos.

The formalities of active or regular military duty—salutes, drills, grooming and so forth—bored me. Also, I felt I was getting away from what really interested me: guerrilla activity in Latin America. Far away from Managua, it was very difficult for us to maintain communication with other organizations of the continent, and even with Argentine colleagues who were there or who were passing through with information from my country.

But there was some excitement. To celebrate the first anniversary of the Sandinista revolution, Fidel traveled to Nicaragua. My stepmother, Conchita, came as part of his delegation. I asked permission to travel to Managua for a few days to see her.

I arrived on July 19 to find that Managua was one big party. We were convinced that a new era was opening up in Latin America. Since the overthrow of Batista, the revolutionary movement had experienced only defeat. But now, when we least expected it, a flame of hope had been ignited in the most unlikely of places—Nicaragua. The message was clear: Cuba was not an exception. Revolution was possible. One year after the fall of the Somoza dictatorship we had proof that the Sandinistas were there to stay.

For that first anniversary, delegations from all of the revolutionary organizations in the Americas had come to Managua. The common topic of conversation was, What would be the next domino in the civil wars then being waged by the left in neighboring countries? Which would fall first, El Salvador or Guatemala? For me it was a heady atmosphere. (I was among those who preferred revolution while it was being waged to revolution once installed.) And I don't know if it was the excitement, or recollections of frontier ennui, or simply that I didn't know how to live any other way, but in the euphoria of the moment I decided that I had to go where the action was. Since I no longer depended on the leadership of my Argentine organization for marching orders, I asked Morejón, the official who had "run" me in Havana, what my next step should be. He advised me to go to Havana and speak with Piñeiro. I left two days later.

About a week after that, I was in Redbeard's office, face to face with my boss and mentor.

We talked for a long time, particularly about the situation in Argentina and in Central America. Then I spelled out my wish to see some real action. He was understanding and said he wanted me to join the Guatemalan Guerrilla Army of the Poor (or EGP in Spanish initials), which was about to launch a general offensive inspired by the Sandinista victory. So it was decided I would go there rather than to El Salvador.

Back in Managua, I met with EGP representatives. They suggested I should travel first to Mexico and from there enter Guatemala with the assistance of their *compañeros*. I spoke with an Argentine friend with a contact in Mexico who could put me up.

With a falsified passport of the worst quality, I left Nicaragua.

8

Mexico City, 1980

"I AM MARTÍN," I SAID TO THE GIRL who was standing in front of a bank in the Mexico City airport. "You're ten minutes late."

She looked at her watch but otherwise seemed unruffled. Accustomed to dealing with brusque and self-important revolutionaries, she did not deign to answer back. She simply requested me to follow her; some friends who had been kind enough—she emphasized the word "kind"—to take her to the airport were waiting outside. At that moment I glanced at her for the first time and saw a stunning pair of chestnut-brown eyes.

When we got to her apartment, I naturally attempted to start up a conversation. Silvia—she told me her name reluctantly—answered every question in monosyllables. Then she said she would call some sympathizers who could put me up while I was in Mexico City. Shamelessly, I claimed that this would create security problems; the *compañeros* had referred me to her and to her alone. I could not possibly go to someone they had not recommended! In addition I had already given them her phone number so they could communicate with me. (That too was a lie—I would never have given out the telephone numbers of the houses where I temporarily stayed.) But at that moment I was willing to seize on any argument that would keep me from having to leave the bewitching eyes.

My obstinacy seemed to persuade her. She soon relaxed and offered me a glass of wine, which I took to be an encouraging sign. I asked her about herself. She confided that she had belonged to the student front of the Argentine guerrillas. Her boyfriend had been kidnapped by the military. She had been forced to go into exile in Mexico where she was studying linguistics. She continued to work on solidarity activities for our country.

I loved talking with Silvia. We had known each other for only two hours and we were already communicating with complete trust. The combination of her eyes and the wine made me feel relaxed and very happy.

Despite my limited budget, I invited her out to dinner. This was a smart move. That night the magic of love touched me once again. Silvia and I thought our affair would last only for a short time because soon I was supposed to leave for Guatemala.

I was to rendezvous with the Guatemalan contact at Sanborn's restaurant in San Angel, a meeting place for political refugees from all over Latin America as well as for members of the Mexican left. An old man who looked like an intellectual appeared right on schedule and gave me the EGP newspaper and a book—*Days in the Jungle* by Mario Payeras—that described the group's origins. He told me that for the moment he could not divulge anything more; I would have to talk with another *compañero* not then in Mexico. We agreed to meet again the next week. Glancing around at the scene, a police informer's paradise, I suggested that we pick a different place.

For the next few days, life with Silvia was marvelous. She introduced me to the secrets of that magical city which, despite its skyscrapers, horrible highways, suffocating air pollution and other unpleasant features, still has an amazing vitality. I imagined that if one day an earthquake were to make the city disappear, a new Aztec civilization might reemerge intact from the ruins.

Every afternoon I picked up Silvia at the university and we went for a walk through Coyoacán. We would stop at the Gandhi bookstore for coffee or have a few glasses of wine with her friends. I was like a schoolboy overcome by youthful discoveries. I let myself be led around, learned to eat foods that were *muy picante,* and found that the best Mexican wines are those that have just come onto the market.

Lying next to Silvia one morning, I read in the newspaper that Somoza had been assassinated in Paraguay. There was no information other than a description of the attack and a suggestion that the operation had been carried out by a group of Argentines. Without a shadow of doubt they were my *compañeros.* The next day there was a photo in all the papers of Skinny Santiago, the only one who had been identified. Two or three days later the news of his death, together with a photo of his body, was published. I felt shame and guilt because I had not been there with him.

Later I discovered that it was he who had been given the job of firing a bazooka at the exiled dictator's armored car. He knelt in the middle of the street facing the oncoming vehicle. His shot hit the mark dead center, but the projectile was a dud. And then, amid the ensuing crossfire, still kneeling alone in the middle of the street, he calmly reloaded and made the second shot that killed Somoza. The guerrillas then hastily withdrew according to plan and dispersed in different directions, throwing away their weapons. Santiago meanwhile, inexplicably, had to find a hiding place on his own. Because of his flaming red beard and hair, he could not easily disappear unnoticed in a city like Asunción: when Santiago went out to buy food, the clerk recognized him and called the police. Surrounded and unarmed, Skinny tried to escape through the patio. The first bullet hit him when he was trying to jump over the well. He was probably only wounded, but two days later when the newspapers published a photo of his body, it was naked, with several bullet holes in his chest just like Che in Bolivia.

AT LAST I HAD THE LONG-AWAITED second contact with the EGP. This time the old gentleman came accompanied by another person. It was Rolando Morán, the "maximum leader" of the organization. I was happy, because I thought his presence at the meeting meant that my departure for Guatemala was imminent.

We talked for a long time. Once again I had to recount my revolutionary resumé, the operations in which I had taken part, and the training I had undergone. For his part, he told me the history of the Guatemalan organization, the sacrifices they had made—which I too would be expected to make. I detected a certain hostility on Rolando's part, but did not pay much attention to it, chalking it up to my ingrained paranoia.

He suggested finally that I must go to Cuba to take a course. At first I refused: I'd been through all that. And I knew perfectly well that you may know when you're going into Cuba but not when you're going to get back out. I had done the courses and it seemed an utterly ridiculous waste of time. But Rolando pointed out that a majority of the guerrillas in Guatemala were Indians and I knew nothing of their culture or customs. He added that at that very moment there was a large group of them living and training in Havana and obvious benefits would accrue if I could spend time with them before going on to their country. I wasn't persuaded. We parted company without seeing eye to eye.

It made no sense. If we had agreed in Managua that I would travel to Mexico and cross into Guatemala from there, why did the

Guatemalans now come to me with this story about the Indians and further delays in Cuba? Were they putting me to the test? Months later I learned that this smoke screen resulted from the fact that Rolando was a close friend of Renán's, the Cuban who ran Nicaraguan intelligence, who had passed on bad reports about me because I had left his operation. Moreover, Renán, who belonged to the Cuban Special Troops, was in open war with Piñeiro's Americas Department. So, although I was completely unaware of it at the time, I was a victim of one of the petty civil wars that always seemed to be taking place in Fidel's court.

The Guatemalans did not reestablish contact because of the backbiting and also because the EGP had carried out a kidnapping in Guatemala that had gone awry: some of their members had been arrested while attempting to collect the ransom in Mexico, obliging their agents in that country to clear out.

For the first time in many years I found myself in the situation of having to face life the way a normal person does. I had to work to make a living, pay for electricity, telephone, rent. Incredible as it may seem, some of these everyday challenges were harder for me to surmount than any clandestine operation. I got a job selling clothes.

I was very happy with Silvia. We decided to have a child.

I had contacted the Popular Liberation Forces (FPL) of El Salvador; I gave courses in covert operations; I had sporadic meetings with the representative of the Americas Department in the Cuban embassy in Mexico City. All in all I had gone from being a revolutionary to being an almost-revolutionary.

I CONTINUED TO LIAISE WITH Jorge Luis Joa, Piñeiro's man in Mexico City. But we rubbed each other the wrong way, perhaps because he represented everything I disliked about the bureaucracy: a mediocre desk-jockey, incapable of making decisions, solely concerned with maintaining his position at the embassy. For my part, I worshipped insolence, mocking his formalities and fears right to his face.

On one occasion I met Joa at the home of a mutual friend, a woman who also worked at the Cuban embassy. He was terrified because Havana had sent him instructions to intervene on behalf of a Colombian who had been arrested in Mexico for using a false passport. This was not just any Colombian, but Jaime Guillot Lara, a well-known drug racketeer and gunrunner, to whom the Cubans owed favors because he had used his narcotics network to run arms into Nicaragua.

As it later transpired, he was a close friend of Fernando Ravelo's, the Cuban ambassador in Colombia, becoming his drug connection.

I was shocked to learn about all this. Along with almost all the other true believers, I naively used to think that the rumors about tie-ups with the drug lords were nothing but imperialist slanders aimed at isolating Cuba. And naively, I asked Joa for more information. Obviously frightened, he blurted out, "I didn't say anything. I don't know what you're talking about."

Ambassador Ravelo himself eventually traveled to Mexico City to handle the negotiations with the Mexican authorities. Guillot Lara left for Spain as a result and from there went on to Cuba, where he died of a heart attack in the mid-1990s. Incredible though it may seem, I was the one slandered in the unraveling of this story. Joa, the frightened functionary, got it into his head to send a report to Cuba accusing me of being in Mexico with the sole motive of robbing banks for my own profit, and recommending that Cuba break all connections with me. This was his devious way of compromising my bona fides and preventing me from informing Piñeiro of the drug rumors I had heard, which might conceivably have led to his being accused of security violations.

With no knowledge of Joa's secret report, I could not understand why the Cubans stopped receiving me. I sought direct contact with Piñeiro, but got no answer. When I asked for a visa to visit Mónica and my children in Havana, I was denied without explanation.

Two or three months went by. Joa was finally removed and replaced by Fernando Comas, whose nom de guerre in Cuba and Nicaragua was "Alejandro." We had been friends for years. As soon as he arrived in Mexico City he got in touch with me. An extended discussion gave me the opportunity to refute the accusations made against me.

I was angry that Piñeiro himself had not called. But Alejandro convinced me that the subject was settled, and we went out to dinner together.

When we met again the following week, Alejandro came with Manolo Orgalles, whom I had also known in Managua, and with whom I was also very friendly. Orgalles was a kind of assistant—and trusted confidant—to both Alejandro and Piñeiro. We had a few drinks and spoke casually about my situation; I let them know that I had few—if any—plans and worked every now and then with the Salvadorans, but without any great commitment.

Alejandro suggested that I stop fooling around and go to work for Cuba once and for all. I was not surprised by the proposition.

According to our worldview, Cuba was not just another foreign country but rather the natural homeland of the world revolutionary movement. Besides, I had been raised in Cuba, and inevitably it would seem like coming home; with the Cubans as my patrons I could help revolutionary efforts everywhere. Alejandro said that in my new job I would be a sort of factotum for Cuba in its relations with the liberation fronts: delivering funds, transporting weapons, looking for safe houses for the leaders, and organizing clandestine meetings.

I was thrilled. Finally I would get back to working on concrete things. The experience in Nicaragua had left me with frustrated ambitions that never quite disappeared, and since then—despite a good relationship with Silvia—I intuited that I was wandering from the path I had chosen many years before. Working with the Cubans would mean coming back to the center of things.

And in my ever-so-intricate family story, my path would once again intersect with my father's.

THE NORMS OF COVERT OPERATIONS dictated that I should stay away from the Cuban embassy. But it was not long before the subterfuge of secret meetings became unnecessarily cumbersome; my upbringing in Cuba and my father's history, in any case, made my presence within the diplomatic compound understandable for the Mexican authorities and did not arouse undue suspicions. My primary difficulty consisted in not having a passport in my own name. It was decided therefore, with a nicely Byzantine maneuver, that I should travel to Havana so they could forge me an Argentine passport in my real name. In addition they procured me a letter from a friendly Peruvian magazine so I could apply for a visa as a foreign correspondent in Mexico—which would give me legal status.

I had never imagined that the climate inside an embassy could be so hostile, above all among the services that were supposedly dedicated to a single cause. Besides us, there were the people from the "center," who worked for the Cuban General Intelligence Agency (the Cuban equivalent of the CIA, known by its Spanish initials as the DGI), and an officer from the operational unit of Special Troops in charge of that agency's relationship with the revolutionary movements. We all worked in theory for the same Revolution, but jealousy and competition provoked unending bureaucratic warfare and constant efforts to trip each other up: after visiting a contact, you would sometimes find his name in the files of all three services.

The files, in fact, require an explanation.

Anyone having the slightest contact with any one of the Cuban intelligence organizations, even unknowingly, had a file opened in which his habits, pleasures, weaknesses, virtues, operational possibilities and relationships would be noted and collated. If it was possible to discover some hidden vice or weakness, so much the better, because someone so compromised could be used. Any acquaintance, without his knowledge, could become a candidate for "agent of influence," to whom attention would be given according to what was thought possible to squeeze from him. Journalists, businessmen, politicians: they were all potential contacts. If they showed the slightest sympathy for the Cuban Revolution, they would be given "the treatment," which consisted of visits to their homes, little gifts of rum and cigars from Cuba, and perhaps, depending on their potential importance, all-expenses-paid trips to Havana. There are many people who would be surprised to see that they had files and to learn that they were Cuban agents without knowing it.

But finding "fellow travelers" was not my preferred area of activity. What interested me was anything that might assist in furthering the revolutionary movements. To this end, I organized protection for meetings between officials of our department and leaders from various allied organizations or countries. This was not a particularly complicated task. It involved arranging to pick up comrades at a certain specific point, then verifying that they were not being followed— and only then allowing them to meet an embassy official. We took measures that made it possible to evade any surveillance that might not have been detected by the usual verification process. On one occasion, people from FAR,* one of the guerrilla organizations operating inside Guatemala, got word to us that they had a substantial quantity of plastic explosives which they had not been able to send home, and that they did not have the secure facilities needed to continue storing them. We immediately thought that these explosives might be useful for the Salvadoran guerrillas and we ordered the Guatemalans to hand the material over to us so that we could put them to good use.

I was supposed to use a certain car to transport these explosives because it was the only one that did not have a diplomatic license plate. I was to leave it parked at a prearranged place and hand over a

---

*FAR—*Fuerzas Armadas Revolucionarias,* or in English, the Revolutionary Armed Forces—had been created by a group of left-wing military officers close to Cuba.

set of keys, also in advance. Later I would pick it up with its cargo and take it to the Cuban embassy.

Everything went according to plan. I arrived at the location and the car was there. Assuming that it was plastic explosives that would not blow up unless detonated, I took no safety precautions. After driving across half of Mexico City, I arrived at the embassy and waited for them to open the enormous metal gate. I parked the car in my assigned spot in the basement and went up to the office to inform Alejandro that the explosives were there and everything had gone fine. When he asked if anything could be seen from outside, I said yes because some of the boxes were on the passenger seat in the back. He asked Manolo and me to bring them upstairs so the other personnel in the embassy couldn't see them.

We brought them up, but since they felt wet while we were carrying them, we opened them up to see what was going on. We were astonished, or more precisely terrified, when we discovered that it wasn't plastique but nitroglycerin in the boxes. Not only was it leaking, but it had even begun to produce little crystals, which the slightest friction could have set off, exploding the entire shipment with enough force to pulverize the embassy and half a block around it.

My fear didn't take long to turn into indignation as I thought about what would have been left of me if my "luggage" had blown up. Alejandro and Manolo were also furious, even more so given that the dangerous cargo was now inside the embassy. While we were thinking about what to do with the goddamn boxes, Alejandro began to smile and wondered aloud what public statements Fidel would have made about the CIA if the Guatemalan rebels' nitroglycerin had demolished our embassy! The affair had an undeniably farcical side to it.

That night, we found a good friend from Chile, José Carrasco, "El Pepone," who stoically agreed to store the explosives in his house and get rid of them little by little. Years later, Pepone returned legally to Chile despite being a known leftist leader, and from within the magazine *Analisis* and the left-wing front organizations he waged a political battle against the Pinochet dictatorship, which eventually had him killed.

My assignments became more and more diverse. In one case I was given the task of getting contacts who would lend us their names to open bank accounts in which we deposited the money earned through an operation we called "the centrifuge." It was based on the fact that every tourist leaving Mexico was allowed to buy five hundred U.S.

dollars with pesos at the official exchange rate. This was about half the black market rate for dollars. So anyone going back to Havana was required to meet Manolo in the airport waiting room where they would give him the U.S. money, and later I would change it on the black market and deposit the proceeds in interest-bearing accounts, from which we would withdraw money to buy dollars again. Since up to twenty-five persons connected with us were flying out of Mexico every week, it will be appreciated that the amount we took in was considerable. It was a way of raising money for our operations over and above the limited official budget we had. Increasingly Havana was pressuring us to scrounge hard currency any way we could.

9

MEXICO CITY, 1982–1983

H AVANA ORDERED US TO HELP THE Latin American groups that operated in Mexico and were supporting their revolutionary activities by staging robberies of everything from banks to jewelry
stores. The man in Cuba who masterminded all of this was
Armando Campos, who worked under Piñeiro as the first deputy
director of the Americas Department.

Because of its porous borders, ineffectual police, large population
and numerous exiles, Mexico presented exceptional advantages. Its
geographical position was also propitious for supporting operations
in neighboring countries. The need was clear: with the Reagan administration now going after them, the majority of the South American
revolutionary organizations were going through difficult times. As
their financial problems grew more and more urgent, crime turned
into a permanent activity. There were comrades who specialized in
this type of revolutionary banditry. These actions conferred power, a
certain glamour, and financial autonomy much greater than the other
militants had, even those who faced the hardships of working underground in their own countries. Whether or not we could make a revolution, we could certainly rob a bank.

These operations had the added advantage of enabling Cuba to
reduce the aid it had to pay out. In addition, as administrator of these
crime-generated funds, Havana accrued power by being able to finance
favored groups, and even by financing the movements of officials of
the Americas Department.

These criminal operations were not at first large-scale. The diplomatic pouch was used to carry the necessary small arms we used in
holdups. As it became clear how lucrative crime could be, Cuba began
to contribute intelligence and even to put groups of different origin

in contact with each other in order to carry out more ambitious projects. Additionally, the Cubans encouraged those revolutionary exiles that were not yet implicated to get into the game.

Our job was to hand over to these groups whatever support came from Havana: weapons, money to mount the operations, air tickets in case anyone had to travel to Cuba. We did not always know (or at least I didn't know) about specific actions in advance. To be sure, once they had been carried out it was difficult not to know because they were sensationally reported on in the press. I recall that one time we supplied weapons to a particular place in Mexico City and a week later two banks on the same corner were robbed. The press opined that because of the level of expertise and the cold-bloodedness of the attackers, this could only be the work of renegade cops. We immediately understood who it really was—which we could confirm a few days later when the person to whom we had handed over the weapons gave us a large sum in blank traveler's checks. And of course he warned us that they weren't clean.

We gave support on another occasion to a group of Macheteros— Puerto Rican independence fighters. I was given the job of hooking up with the militants who traveled to Mexico for an operation. The description of the contact had been quite sketchy. I was to wait for him at the entrance of a movie theater on Reforma Street. All I knew was that he would be carrying a rolled-up newspaper in his right hand. By chance the time of the appointment coincided with the time the movie ended. There was a large audience, and many of them left the theater with newspapers in their right hands. I decided to wait until the place cleared out a little. Finally I noticed a man leaning against a pillar. Without being very certain that he was the one I was waiting for, I approached to ask him a question. I wanted him to speak so I could verify his accent. I heard an unmistakable Puerto Rican lilt.

"Junior," as he introduced himself, was thin and tall, kinetic in his nervousness. He had two reasons for contacting us. He wanted us to put him in touch with a Chilean who could give him a course in electronics so the Macheteros could transmit "outlaw" television propaganda back home. Then he wanted us to loan him $50,000 until his group could carry out a job that they were preparing in the United States.

I went everywhere with my new Puerto Rican friend until the day finally arrived for him to be turned over to the Chilean, who was demanding security measures so extreme that they'd draw the attention of the police. First, I had to honk the horn of my car below his apartment. Second, we had to stand in front of the place so he could observe us from the window. Finally, we had to take the elevator to the top floor of his old building, then go down the stairs to his floor, knock three times on his door and identify ourselves with a stupid phrase. Only then would he open up. When Alejandro spelled out these requirements I started to laugh, thinking it was a joke. He told me seriously: "If you don't, he won't let you in. He's one of the biggest jerks I've ever encountered."

Imagine my surprise when, after I had scrupulously followed these ridiculous instructions, the door opened and I discovered before me a man I knew—a man who, years before, had proved himself a coward by abandoning his commander in mid-battle, running away without making the slightest effort to protect one of the most honest and capable revolutionary leaders of our generation. I could not understand how the Cubans would use such a person on delicate missions.

His first words when he opened the door were: "Did you make sure that no one followed you?" I had to conceal my disgust. I left the Puerto Rican with him and went immediately to the embassy to complain to Alejandro. I didn't want to have anything more to do with the Chilean. If he had abandoned his own leader, he could just as easily betray me.

The course on electronics lasted a week. When it ended, I went to pick up Junior and took him to live in my house; we had to wait until the $50,000 was delivered from Havana before he could go home. I used the time to package the television transmitter and ready it for shipment. Two or three days later José Antonio Arbesú, head of the United States section of the Americas Department, and another Cuban official who worked with him, called Arana, arrived with the money.

To transport the money I modified a piece of Samsonite luggage, taking the riveting off the top, placing the cash between the top and the lining made out of fabric and cardboard, then putting it back together. Since we didn't know if the X-ray machines in the airports could detect paper, we bought a second identical suitcase so that the Puerto Rican could take it empty through immigration. My comrade Manolo would have the job of going through with the full suitcase, thanks to his diplomatic passport. All Junior would have to do was sit next to Manolo in the waiting area and switch the suitcases. Thus Junior would leave with a suitcase full of money and a portable television with the transmitter concealed inside that we checked through to Puerto Rico for him.

Months later—in September 1983—the Macheteros assaulted a Wells Fargo armored car in the United States and took more than $7 million in loot—$7.1 million, to be exact. At the time I was in Argentina, but I immediately remembered how, when he was with us, Junior had kept asking if we knew of any powerful sleeping pill that coffee might be spiked with, and how he chattered on about the interiors of armored cars.

I don't know if they used sleeping pills to put the driver or the guard to sleep. What I do know is that they had an accomplice inside the armored car, because three months after the robbery, Alejandro called me in Buenos Aires asking me to hurry back to Mexico to help prepare an operation.

When I arrived, it was explained that they needed me because $4 million from the Macheteros' robbery had to be picked up on the border to be sent on, via Mexico, to Havana in a diplomatic pouch. They also asked me to help them procure Argentine documents for the accomplice in the robbery, a Puerto Rican named Víctor Gerena, who at that time was in Mexico under the embassy's protection. Then we helped smuggle him to Cuba.

This story had its epilogue many years later, in 1999, when President Bill Clinton caused a furor by reducing the sentences of a group of Macheteros jailed in the United States. One of them, I had learned, was "Junior"—real name Juan Segarra Palmer—who had been caught and convicted on charges stemming from the robbery.

Thus did Cuban intelligence organize and finance the largest cash robbery in U.S. history.

SOMETIMES DIFFICULT INDIVIDUALS came our way from Havana. The most annoying of them all was Ramiro Abreu, the man in charge of Central America for the Americas Department. He had a reputation as something of a genius—a reputation he himself had helped spread—because of the aid he had delivered to the Sandinistas during their war against Somoza. But my experience of his genius had nothing to do with revolutionary struggle and everything to do with the ingenious inventiveness of his excuses for making shopping trips to Mexico.

Once he came to buy a medicine cabinet for his bathroom. But not just any medicine cabinet; it was one his wife had requested. She had even drawn a sketch of the model, which had to have interior lights. It fell to me to take Abreu all over Mexico City trying to find the item. After five hours on the absurd expedition, the likes of which I had never before experienced, we found something similar to what he was looking for. Back in the embassy, we wrapped it up so that Abreu could easily carry it on the plane. The next day he returned to Havana, his revolutionary duty completed.

Imagine our surprise when, a few days later, we received a telegram from Abreu, giving us the measurements of one of the mirrors in the medicine cabinet and asking us to look for one just like it because the original had broken on the trip. We did what he asked, but a week later he sent the mirror back because it didn't fit right and added a note specifying the measurements in greater detail. This time we didn't try very hard. About ten days later, Abreu concocted an imaginary meeting with revolutionary exiles and came back to Mexico City, medicine cabinet and all. He had gone so far as to buy the cabinet a round-trip ticket so it could travel on the seat next to him and the mirror would not again be in danger. Naturally he didn't pay for the tickets himself, because they were part of a quota that Cubana Airlines gave the Americas Department for the aid of liberation movements.

Even worse than Abreu were those within the embassy who devoted themselves to spying on the rest of the personnel and sending secret reports to Cuba. For them, everything was important—a gesture, a comment, amorous relationships. Fortunately I was a foreigner under the orders of Alejandro and, in the final analysis, of Piñeiro. I did not live in Cuba, nor was I a member of the Communist Party. Hence I escaped much of this spying, which was a good thing considering my weakness for "bourgeois" pleasures.

A FEW MONTHS AFTER I STARTED WORKING for the Cubans, Alejandro's deputy, "Chino Igor," arrived from Havana. At first we were happy because we had a lot of work to do and another colleague was really necessary. But when we got to know him, we realized our mistake: he was unbearable. On one occasion, I had to take him to a meeting with a Guatemalan guerrilla leader, a man who had just left his country and come in illegally from the mountains. In the car, El Chino began to ask him about the internal situation in his country and the *compañero* explained to him with great clarity the difficulties of the situation, but stressed they were still making every effort to move ahead in the war. El Chino interrupted and arrogantly criticized him. Assuming the air of a *comandante,* he pushed methods such as those described in obsolete manuals of irregular warfare—this while riding in a comfortable, air-conditioned vehicle protected by diplomatic license plates. I could not believe what I was hearing and I looked at the Guatemalan with shame. At one point, I thought I noted a certain complicity in his expression, as if he were saying to me, "Just let him talk—he's an idiot."

On another occasion, Piñeiro traveled to Mexico City to meet with President Miguel de la Madrid. Nothing appeared in the press about this visit. Piñeiro did not ordinarily travel abroad; he came to Mexico only because its intelligence service was so closely linked to Cuba's. Despite the official escort provided by the Mexican authorities, we were entrusted with his security. We accepted the job eagerly—we had little faith in the Mexican police.

Before his arrival, we allocated responsibilities. Manolo would go in the lead car with a member of Piñeiro's escort who came from Havana. Alejandro would be in the same car as Piñeiro, with the ambassador's driver. El Chino would follow immediately after to prevent the Mexican police from taking that spot. Only at the end of the convoy would the police be allowed to take position. Behind them, very discreetly, I and another Argentine *compañero* who used to help us would follow with two pistols and a submachine gun in case there was a clash and we had to help Piñeiro's vehicle escape.

Everything was perfectly planned. As soon as Piñeiro's car left the airport on the highway to Polanco, everyone moved into place. We had hardly driven ten minutes in dense traffic when we found ourselves next to El Chino. I thought his car was having mechanical problems and I quickly gestured to my Argentine companion to move ahead and get us between the Mexican police car and Piñeiro any way he could. Fortunately the screw-up had no consequences and we arrived at the ambassador's house, where Piñeiro was staying, without any problems. I told Alejandro what had happened. Even then, El Chino had not yet arrived and we were worried about his delay.

A little later he appeared, looking as if nothing were amiss. His explanation was that he had gotten lost because he didn't know the way, but that was impossible because we took that route every other day, whenever a flight came in from Cuba. He had simply been nervous. He did not lack for courage when advising the Guatemalans, but on a simple escort mission he ran scared.

The three days of Piñeiro's visit were exhausting. We not only had to guard him when he was moving, but we also had to watch the house. I didn't get a chance to talk to him until his last day. He asked me with great interest about the support we were giving to the groups that were hunting for money in Mexico City, and he said I should devote myself more to that role. He advised me to search for bigger targets, because the smalltime bank heists did not bring in enough to justify their extreme riskiness.

The bank robberies did intensify and, curiously, we had no security problems, at least not until the Mexican police detained a group from Cuban intelligence that was supposed to make contact with a rogue CIA agent who was allegedly going to give them information. The best idea they could come up with was to set the appointment for a downtown hotel, near where President Miguel de la Madrid was scheduled to give a speech. Even worse, they were carrying with them a small suitcase equipped with a self-destruct mechanism capable of destroying the enclosed documents if someone tried to pick the lock. Upon arriving at the hotel, they were arrested by the Mexican police, who had been told that a briefcase bomb would be used to sabotage the president's speech. It was a provocation arranged by the CIA, which only worked because of the lack of professionalism on the part of the Cubans. But then, on top of everything else, the arrested agents told their interrogators that their boss was Fernando Comas, Alejandro's legal name. By so doing, they were not only trying to cover for their own agency, but also, along the way, settling some old scores from the little internal wars between the Cuban services. As a consequence, the Mexican authorities put Alejandro under observation along with our entire team. We were forced to cut back on the number of operations we could do, and carried out only the indispensable missions. For the Mexican police we had become undesirables.

I was the weakest link in the chain because I was the only one who didn't have diplomatic immunity. I became the favorite target of provocations. One night, upon arriving home with Silvia, I got out of the car to open the garage door and someone in a passing car fired two shots into the air. I was armed, but just in time I spotted another car parked in front, with three guys inside who looked like police. I didn't even think of drawing my weapon: that's exactly what they were waiting for so they would have an excuse to arrest me or shoot me on the spot.

I went to the embassy early next day to tell Alejandro what had happened, but he did not ascribe much importance to it. That very afternoon, I can't remember for what reason, Manolo accompanied me home. No sooner had we stepped out of the car than the events of the night before were repeated. We returned immediately to the embassy and this time it was Manolo who told Alejandro the story. The next day I was on a plane for Havana.

10

HAVANA–LIMA–SANTA CRUZ, SEPTEMBER 1983

U PON MY ARRIVAL IN HAVANA I discovered that elections would be held in Argentina. It was a historic event. These would be the first elections since the military coup of 1976. I wanted to go home immediately. It's hard to explain why. Perhaps I thought that if I awaited the arrival of democracy and returned legally, the military would have inflicted a personal defeat upon me.

This time my conversation with Piñeiro lasted a long time. I told him how things had gone in Mexico and, in broad outline, how I wanted to return to my country. Piñeiro didn't think much of the chances for a stable democracy in Argentina and predicted that it would have a short life before the military returned to the scene. (As it transpired, of course, this was a wish-fulfilling fantasy.) His advice to me and my *compañeros* was to continue preparations for military struggle and be ready to act when democracy collapsed. I was in agreement, not because I wanted a harsh militarism to struggle against, but simply because of the historical fact that in my country, for the last thirty years, only two civilian governments had been able to complete their terms, whereas all the others had been brought down by military coups.

Piñeiro told me to stay in touch because I might need his help. He put me in contact with an official I hadn't met yet, Antonio López, who also worked with Armando Campos on operational issues, so that we could establish a protocol for communications and he could provide me with some intelligence relating to the Argentine military.

Finally, I had a farewell meeting with Piñeiro. Once more, we traced my itinerary. I would leave Havana for Lima, go from Peru to Rio de Janeiro, and from there to the Argentine border to enter at the Iguazú Falls. There I would destroy my passport and use the identity card I myself had made a month before. He gave me plane tickets and $6,000 to get started in Argentina. He asked me to let him know my location as soon as I had a place because he would have things for me to do.

I ARRIVED IN LIMA AT FIVE in the afternoon. I think this is the saddest time of day in that city. Is it because of the evening fog, or the leaden gray sky? I don't know. But from the moment I entered the outskirts I became deeply depressed, so much so that even though I customarily stroll through the markets in a new town or have a beer in some lively bar, that time I went directly to a cheap little hotel and stayed there in my room reading until I fell asleep.

At dawn, I went to the airport to board the plane for Rio, but at the last moment I decided not to travel to Brazil and instead asked for a ticket to Santa Cruz, Bolivia, with a change of planes in La Paz. Many comrades had already used the border crossing at Iguazú and it was possible that it could be already "burned."

Landing in Santa Cruz, I found myself standing at the tiny airport holding my carry-on bag, without the slightest idea of how to get to the border or where to make the best crossing into Argentina. I walked through the city and went to a bar. There I obtained information from some locals about a train that would pass by within three days. They also told me that the only air connection to Argentina was through the town of Salta and it would leave that very afternoon. I decided against the plane because I was too unsure of the quality of my passport to risk the immigration check. As I chatted further with my fellow barflies, one of them explained to me that if I wanted to leave for Argentina that afternoon, I should take the "mobility"—a bus that picked people up at the highway crossroads. In the city of Camiri, I could find something that would take me to the border.

When I got to the intersection, people were already waiting for the "mobility." Most were Indians who were transporting merchandise. With my light blue striped suit and my rather loud red tie, a passable getup for travel by plane but not for waiting at a dusty roadside, I felt pretty ridiculous—even more so when the "mobility" appeared. At first I had not worried about the name. If in Mexico they called a bus a "truck," in Nicaragua simply "bus," and in Cuba "*guagua*," why shouldn't people in Bolivia call it a "mobility"? But what I saw coming down the road was not a bus, it was a cargo truck crammed full of Indians with their possessions, including chickens. I had no choice but to enjoy the ridiculousness of the situation, so I took off my jacket and tie and climbed into the truck along with all the people and barnyard animals.

The trip was interminable: eleven hours to Camiri over a dirt road with only one stop to eat. And when we finally made that stop, I thought I wouldn't be able to stand up. Six hours seated in the same position—because the volume of people and packages prevented any movement—had been torture. The idea of at least eating something revived me. But my joy didn't last long. The only thing available was greasy tripe and some boiled vegetables. I ate only the vegetables, but the repugnant odor of the tripe followed me during the entire rest of the trip—another five hours.

Camiri felt like a ghost town. The ground was dry, giving off an atrocious dust that colored everything a dull yellow. At first I couldn't see a single person, just some very skinny dogs with particularly sad eyes. Then I began to make out some faces, and they all—the children, the women, the elderly—had the same look of hungry curiosity. After walking for a long time I found a very poor hotel, if you could call it that, made of adobe bricks. I washed up in the bathroom, removing the layers of dirt I had picked up on my miserable voyage. I also took the opportunity to change clothes. I put on blue jeans and a T-shirt, so that I could pass for a tourist, the only way to justify my presence in the area.

I preferred not to spend the night there, especially since there was no public transportation to take me to the border the next day. After talking with several people, I managed to find a man who was leaving that afternoon in his jeep for Yacuiba, next to Positos on the Bolivian side (on the other side was the Argentine town also called Positos), and for a few pesos he agreed to take me.

We left at the approach of night. Since this journey was more comfortable than the last, I could appreciate the beauty of the place. To the west in the distance I could make out some immense mountains. I supposed they were the very same ones where Che himself had wandered before he met his end, and I felt a powerful emotion. Also, upon actually entering Argentina, I knew I would pass very close to the area where my father had died. Again our paths were crossing. I asked the driver if he knew anything about Che.

"Yes," he said, nodding toward the mountains. "The guerrillas went around over there during the war."

He didn't say any more. We continued the journey in silence.

When we arrived, the man offered to take me to Positos for a few more pesos, which I immediately accepted. The border was now closed and I couldn't find anywhere to spend the night. I decided to wait about two hundred meters from the border crossing, in a place where I could observe every movement. I was still worried about the poor quality of my passport. I decided to destroy it. Now, there was no turning back. My identity card worked only for crossing between neighboring countries. If I didn't make it to Argentina, I'd be stuck in Bolivia.

At around four in the morning, I saw a group of about ten people crossing over. But rather than going through the border post, they were taking a road about fifty meters away. The officer on guard did not so much as look at them. I regretted not having been closer so as to be able to mix in with them, but consoled myself with the thought that they were surely workers or smugglers who crossed routinely. About ten minutes later, I saw another group that was approaching, headed in the same direction. I went up to them and, saying nothing and trying to hide my bag from the view of the officer, who was not even looking at us, I entered my country once again.

IT HAD BEEN SO EASY! All that was left for me to do now was to make it to the capital. I would take a bus from Positos to Salta, and from there a plane to Buenos Aires. On Argentine domestic flights there is no passport control.

I caught the bus at 6:30 the next morning, and as soon as I took my seat I fell asleep. God knows what I was dreaming about when I was awakened by a slap on the shoulder. It was a police officer who courteously asked me for my identification. I gave him my identity card, not without a certain apprehension, but the officer hardly looked at it, contenting himself with verifying that I was the man in the photograph. I breathed easy. However, when the police finished looking over the documents of all of the passengers, they asked us to get off the bus with all our luggage.

They searched us one by one and, when it was my turn, they instructed me to step to one side. I had to follow them to an office where they searched my bag inch by inch. At the end they ordered me to take off all my clothes, which they examined stitch by stitch, and then hit the heels of my shoes to verify that nothing was hidden in them. One who seemed to be the boss asked me where I came from and what I was doing around there. I responded that I was on vacation and wanted to get to know the north of the country.

Apologetically, he said: "We're not used to seeing people like you around here. But many come looking for cocaine from Bolivia. You may continue."

This brush with authority kept me from sleeping the rest of the trip. I made it to Salta and went directly to the offices of Aerolíneas Argentinas, but there was no flight available until next day. I decided to go find some empanadas and check myself into a good hotel. After killing some time watching local television, I fell asleep. The next morning, we took off from the airpark—as the Argentines call it— and soon I saw Buenos Aires again.

I went immediately to an area where there are what the city's residents call "little cars on the riverbank." Long ago there were trucks on the riverbank that sold roast sausages with bread; later the businesses expanded and they began to sell a complete mixed grill; by the time of my visit the "little cars" had become elegant restaurants. I headed for one of them, called The Crazy Years, which had been my favorite.

After eating a large mixed grill washed down with good Argentine red wine, I lifted my bag onto my shoulder and took a walk along the bank. I surprised myself by whistling a tango. It seemed to me that the river flowed to the same rhythm as the dance. The tango could only have been born in Buenos Aires, and I'm sure that the first tango was composed on a humid summer afternoon on the riverbank.

I arrived at the home of some of Silvia's relatives, who were waiting for me. Before my departure from Mexico, we had asked if they could put me up, so there were no surprises. From the point of view of security, it was ideal because the family had no political connections. They treated me like a son and with great affection.

I established contact with *compañeros* from my organization—or, to put it more precisely, my traveling companions, because politically we were nothing anymore. We agreed to meet in Buenos Aires every Saturday at noon in the Torino Pizzeria. I chose the place because it was near my grandmother's house.

The first Saturday I went there without much hope of meeting anyone, since the persons I had to see were coming from abroad and it was possible they had not yet arrived. As I was asking for the check so I could leave, I saw my mother go by on the sidewalk. I almost ran after her, but I controlled myself. I knew I shouldn't call attention to myself. Many *compañeros* had been taken as they met up with family members.

I had not seen my mother since 1974. Those had been harsher times. Now there was almost no surveillance; the military was in retreat and in two months there would be elections. Besides, I had still not contacted anyone and the police couldn't know that I was in Argentina.

I swiftly left the pizzeria. I tried to saunter nonchalantly, but I couldn't help myself and broke into a run for grandmother's house. She herself came out to answer the door. She looked much older. I hadn't changed much, but I had a very short haircut, and to disguise my face somewhat I was wearing eyeglasses.

"I'm looking for Señora María Jury," I told her very seriously, thinking she would recognize me immediately.

"Who are you?" she asked.

"Your grandson," I said.

She almost fainted. She immediately embraced me and kissed me as only a grandmother can.

I went into the dining room where my mother and my Aunt Yolanda were sitting. My mother was so moved she could not get up. My aunt embraced me and looked at me with astonishment. My grandmother went to the kitchen and came back with a bottle of wine and some cups.

"For my Turk," she said, pouring the wine.

She was the only one who called me "Turk." That's what she also used to call my grandfather because his family was from Lebanon, when it was still part of the old Ottoman Empire.

We made a toast. My mother took me by the hand and gazed at me with great tenderness. Then they wanted to call the whole family on the phone. At first I declined, but then I agreed on condition that they would only call my sister and my Uncle Adolfo, without telling them I was there.

When my sister saw me, she burst into tears.

"I thought I would never see you again," she said.

Then Uncle Adolfo came in asking, "Where is Jorge?"

He had figured out what was up when he heard the emotion in my mother's voice on the telephone.

It was just like when I was a boy—everyone gathered around the table. We talked and laughed. But within a couple of hours, old family quarrels had reignited. This, too, I enjoyed. Around ten at night we said goodbye to one another. I had experienced many emotions all mixed together. I promised to return, visiting them individually at their homes.

On this single day, I had violated more security measures than in all the past years.

I kept on visiting my family, just as I had promised. On the eve of the elections, a new climate of freedom reigned, and unless you got involved in compromising situations, there were few risks.

Taking only minimal precautions, I began to look up other old contacts and friends. I saw that underneath the eagerness to vote, something had changed profoundly. The military terror had left a mark. Even the vocabulary was different. No one spoke of a military dictatorship, but rather of "the process." Not of guerrillas, but rather "the subversion." The mothers of the Plaza de Mayo, who had so dramatically protested the "disappearance" of their children and husbands, were now the "crazy women."

We who had returned were part of a troubling past, and for some we were part of the problem. The "theory of the two evils," which depicted the military and the guerrillas as two sides of the same coin, had taken root. If the guerrillas had not provoked them, the theory held, the military would never have left the barracks. Our defeat was deeper than I could possibly have imagined. "We hope you haven't come back to do the same thing as before," some of my old comrades said.

Political discourse was cramped, ostentatiously "realistic" and, above all, intolerant of utopias. People spoke of democracy without being very clear about what it consisted of, and to add modifiers such as "popular" or "participatory" was regarded as almost subversive.

The labor movement, which had been a social force for the last forty years, was in a state of disarray because the Peronist party no longer represented it. It had become fragmented and disorganized. The Peronists, despite their internal contradictions, had given labor its political identity, but now they had no leaders who enjoyed popularity, much less who were capable of representing the workers.

The Radical Party candidate, Raúl Alfonsín, an honest but limited man, was young, cautious, moderate, dispassionate. These were the virtues of the moment. The Peronist candidate, Italo Luder, surrounded by a terrible Mafia and even by certain collaborators with the dictatorship, was passé. The left was totally splintered; some groups tried to form alliances, but there was no one to ally with. The guerrilla organizations had been annihilated.

What a difference from the elections of 1973! Back then, there had been dreams, utopias and passions. The street belonged to the youth, to the workers, to the students. Che Guevara smiled at us from thousands of posters, as if he were returning to life in his own country.

It was hard for me to adapt to the new situation. Participating in political arguments felt awkward. Those few people who listened to me did so out of nostalgia. The *compañeros* who had returned in secret at the same time as I all had the same experience.

We had been marginalized.

As expected, Alfonsín won. I heard the election results at the home of some friends of Silvia's relatives. People were celebrating in the streets. But they were not my people.

I'll never forget the sight of a man who appeared in the middle of the tumult, totally drunk and wrapped in a wrinkled and dirty Argentine flag. He shouted defiantly: "Long live Perón, goddammit!"

The people shoved him and laughed.

Through a lawyer friend, I initiated the paperwork to obtain my legal identity papers. Fortunately, there were no charges pending against me, in spite of the fact that I was on police intelligence lists and there was an arrest warrant. Instead of starting a lawsuit in which I would have had to explain where I had been and how I came into the country, the simplest thing by far was to bribe a policeman known to my family who had access to the lists, so he would take me off and clear the way to getting the documents.

This matter resolved, I rented an apartment. At the same time, I began to communicate with the Cubans, which was easier now that I had acquired legal status. Then one day I received a message from Alejandro, asking me to return to Mexico. I acquired a legal passport, with some delay but without great inconvenience.

The job with the Cubans was quickly achieved, because most of it was already done even before I arrived; it was a simple a matter of documentation, which didn't take more than a week.

I returned to Argentina, happy and legal, bringing Silvia and my son home with me.

11
Buenos Aires, 1984–1985

IT WAS INCREDIBLE TO CROSS BORDERS and pass through Argentine airport controls in the company of my wife and son, with a legal passport in my own name and without the slightest worry. Things were almost too normal.

I managed to get a job as a production assistant in a feature film. The director had been a good friend of my father's and he accepted me into his crew even though I had no experience in movies. As a production assistant I was able to do some of the publicity. I finally got work at the newspaper *La Voz*, where I soon had a weekly political column and wrote daily for the international section.

I kept in touch with the *compañeros*, but now we were merely friends, not co-conspirators. We discussed politics and life in general. Some of them joined one or another of the various parties on the left and others got into social work in the poorer neighborhoods. I was not attracted to either role. Silvia had a job too; we did well, or at least as well as Argentina permitted in those years of runaway inflation.

My other three children who had been in Cuba also came back to Argentina with their mother, Mónica. We visited each other on the weekends. Silvia got pregnant again and we awaited my fifth child.

The far-reaching change in my life was too abrupt. I was comfortable, but I felt that nothing I was doing was important. I suffered through long periods of depression and began to drink heavily. I wondered if I could keep going without my revolutionary faith. Soon—almost consciously—I was busy destroying everything that I had and most loved.

To this day I am ashamed of what I put Silvia through in that period: drunk all the time, I would come home late without any explanation. That's how I lived my life "after the Revolution." Many people tried to help me, but I was too insensitive to accept their sympathy. I had convinced myself that I was not cut out for ordinary life.

I spent a year and a half this way, squandering my relationship with Silvia and others. Then one day a leader of the Chilean MIR (Movement of the Revolutionary Left) named Pablo made contact with me. I had known him in Mexico, when the MIR was fighting the Pinochet dictatorship. Now he asked for my help with two militants who had to pass through Buenos Aires secretly. I immediately remembered something Piñeiro had said in our last conversation—that I should help Chileans if I ever got a chance—and I told Pablo that he could count on me. After we finished the task at hand, I asked him to keep me in mind for other missions, perhaps some within Chile itself.

A couple of months later Pablo reappeared. He told me that his group needed to buy weapons and asked me to start looking for sellers. I felt reborn. I was finally going to be able to do something for the Revolution again. A few days later I located some pistols and submachine guns. Just a few days before finalizing the purchase, Pablo admitted that the MIR was going through a serious internal crisis and that the section of its leadership that managed the money had frozen the funds. Many militants who were still inside Chile and living undercover were going through a very difficult and dangerous period, especially Nelson Gutiérrez, the charismatic leader of the MIR. He thought it would be a good idea if I went to Havana to explain the situation to Piñeiro and to see if he could procure them the necessary cash for the weapons. When I got back I would travel to Chile with him. I quit the newspaper and left for Havana once again.

One of Piñeiro's officials was waiting for me at the airport. He took me to the hotel and told me to stay where I could be reached; the boss would see me that night. Around nine the phone rang. It was Joel, his chauffeur. He was coming to get me.

Piñeiro's offices were in the headquarters of the Central Committee. There was no security check. We went right inside. Piñeiro was waiting for me at his desk, which was piled high with papers. After a warm greeting, our conversation went to the subject of the situation in Argentina. We had both changed our point of view since our last encounter. The democracy in Argentina was much more stable than we had imagined. Alfonsín, without being a revolutionary or pretending to be one, had put the military high command on trial—those responsible for the tortures and disappearances during the dictatorship. There had been a conviction.

We agreed that it was time to emphasize political—that is, non-violent—forms of struggle. I confessed to him my limitations in this respect and indeed, my lack of interest in legal activities. He advised me to keep assisting the Chilean MIR but to be very careful, because the Argentine secret service could still be watching me.

I told Piñeiro about the internal situation of the MIR, as Pablo had described it. He said that he knew about it more or less and that he was worried about the possibility of a division, but was still optimistic because the differences, he thought, were not fundamental, and the internal schism had yet to become public. I did not share his optimism because experience had taught me to believe that when an organization indulges in this type of internecine rivalry it is difficult to maintain unity.

As for the problem of financial aid, he seemed a bit surprised at this, because he had not been aware that the difficulties had gotten so out of hand. Besides, that raised a delicate problem for him, because, as he explained, the last agreement he had made with the MIR determined that all resources sent out from Cuba had to be channeled through Pascal Allende, the nephew of Salvador and general secretary of the organization, who belonged to the faction in disagreement with Nelson Gutiérrez. He told me he would think about it and talk to Armando Campos, vice chief of the Americas Department.

Next morning, Armando called me and summoned me to an immediate appearance before the Central Committee.

"There's a solution to every problem," he said when I got there. "If we can't give money directly to Pablo because of Allende, we can give it to you for some hypothetical project in Argentina. If you then decide to give it to him, that's your business. We have nothing to do with it. All we can give you is $30,000."

I would not personally courier the money because if I was searched, I would not be able to explain why I had so much cash on me. It would be handed to me by an official of the Cuban embassy in Buenos Aires.

By the time I returned, however, the arms deal I had negotiated had fallen apart. Since our contact had by now been burned, I was forced to go to other, less fruitful sources and buy the weapons in small quantities, in some cases one by one. They actually didn't cost much and I piled them up fairly rapidly.

Meanwhile, Pablo had returned to Chile. A short time later I got a call from the woman whom he had established as his Buenos Aires contact. She told me that when I went to Chile I would have to carry

Top left: My father, Jorge Ricardo Masetti, founder of the Cuban press agency La Prensa Latina, here next to Fidel Castro in 1959–60, when the Revolution was young. Top right: My father with his friend and fellow Argentine Che Guevara. Above: In 1962, my father was back in Cuba during the Missile Crisis just before leaving for Argentina to organize the guerrilla action in which he was killed in April 1964.

MINISTERIO DEL INTERIOR
Managua

SE HACE CONSTAR QUE EL COMPAÑERO "MARTIN", PERTE-
NECE AL MINISTERIO DEL INTERIOR, Y ESTAN AUTORIZA-
DO A REALIZAR LAS TAREAS PROPIAS DE ESTE MINISTE-
RIO, POR LO QUE SE RUEGA A LAS AUTORIDADES CIVILES
Y MILITARES, BRINDARLE LA COLABORACION NECESARIA.

MANAGUA. D

EJERCITO POPULAR SANDINISTA

A , Autoridades Civiles y Militares

DE , Seco. Tropas Guarda Fronteras

ASUNTO: PERMISO PARA PORTAR ARMA

FECHA Junio 9, de 1980.

Por este medio se autoriza al Compañero
Jorge Ricardo Masetty, Jefe de Operaciones
de la Sub-Seco. Tropas Guarda Fronteras, -
de la VII Región Militar, para portar Arma Stikin, AC.1605K, 9 mm. corto con 5 car
gadores. El se dirige a la VII Región.
Agradeciendo la atención que le brinden al
Compañero, me suscribo revolucionariamente

SILVIO CASCO
Asistente del Ministro

EMBAJADA DE LA REPUBLICA DE CUBA
MEXICO, D. F.

The photo of me above was taken in Italy in 1977. In 1979 I was given identity papers by the Sandinista government. Below, another passport photo taken of me in 1980 when I was working with Cuban intelligence in Mexico City. Right: Recruited by the Ministry of the Interior, I was in Angola in 1989.

Top: The twins Patricio and Tony de la Guardia were my comrades in arms and adoptive fathers. Here they are in Paris in 1988, a year before their undoing. Patricio is on the left and Tony on the right, with a bodyguard in between. Middle: Here are the twins' parents, the heads of the de la Guardia family, Graciela and Mario. Above: This snapshot was taken on February 12, 1989, the day Ileana and I were married. She is at left and the friends who helped us celebrate stand beside me under the omnipresent Che. Five months later, Tony would stand in front of a Cuban firing squad next to General Arnaldo Ochoa.

Just before his execution on July 13, 1989, Tony de la Guardia wrote his last letter. The photo at top shows Tony with Ileana in 1986. The second shows me with Ileana in Paris in 1993.

along documents containing the MIR leadership's resolutions about the military policy of the group. My first action, she said, would be to carry out surveillance for an operation in the upper-class Santiago neighborhood of Los Condes. She wanted me to use a Chilean identity card and leave directly from Argentina so as to save money. I said no. To leave Buenos Aires with the Chilean documents seemed crazy to me, because if I was being watched by the Argentine services—as I assumed I was—I might be arrested at the airport and have no defense. I proposed traveling with my legal passport to Uruguay; since it was a neighboring country, you could go in with identity papers and they would give you an entry certificate. I could use the false documents with which I had once entered Argentina. Later, I would claim that my entry certificate had been lost; they would give me another bearing my false name, and with this document I would travel to Chile. I would also take the Chilean identity card—just in case.

All I needed was a way to hide the MIR's secret military documents. This was nothing original: a simple notebook with leather covers thick enough to conceal the photographic negatives of the material.

I left for Chile via Uruguay.

As soon as I arrived in Uruguay, I called some friends who had a trading company. I asked them if they would lend me some of their company's letterhead and then ordered up some business cards identifying me as a commercial representative of the firm. Their office secretary at the same time got me an appointment with the commercial attaché from the Chilean embassy. I went there, presented my cards, and told him of my interest in traveling to Chile to set up a business importing canned juices. Could he possibly provide me with a list of export companies for these products? To reassure him of my bona fides, I gave him the telephone number of the trading office so that he could contact me there. My friends, for their part, agreed to confirm that I was a sales manager for them if someone called from Chile asking for references. The next day he telephoned me and set up an appointment for noon. When I arrived he gave me an extensive list of business contacts in Santiago and his own personal letter of recommendation.

Assuming the identity of a young businessman, I entered Chile through the International Airport in Santiago. I took a bus downtown and, since it was already quite late, went to the first cheap hotel I could find. I spent the next day looking for another one, in a better area near the Salvador Metro station, and visited some of the companies on the list.

You could see the heavy police presence in the streets. They were armed with rifles, and posted at all the exits of the Metro stations and on the street corners. Some were dressed in civilian clothes, but had the unmistakable look of policemen nonetheless. I was surprised that there were no significant identity checks, considering that it was a country under a dictatorship. One could move about freely and this, rather than make me happy, worried me, because it was a sure sign they had infiltrated the revolutionary organizations and did not need to carry out indiscriminate shakedowns. The police presence was to intimidate, not to arrest.

Curfew in Santiago began at 1:00 A.M. It was only for automobiles, so you could still move about on foot. Still, there was a terrible silence, sometimes interrupted by the sound of a car that could only belong to the police. In such moments, the only thing you could hope for was that the vehicles would not stop in front of your door.

I spent the next day visiting producers of canned juice. At five in the afternoon I went to meet with my contact to hand over the document. I arrived on time and did my best to display the visual countersign. Then I saw Pablo himself coming toward me, looking great, smiling as always. We exchanged a few words and agreed to see each other next day at Viña del Mar, a little more than an hour away from Santiago. We met there and took a bus to Valparaiso, one of the most beautiful cities I had ever seen. At an old bar we ordered a bottle of pisco and talked for five hours. Rather than make plans, we fantasized about the future and celebrated being in Chile together.

We continued to meet in different places, and I began learning about the internal situation of the MIR so I could report to Piñeiro on my next trip to Havana. Later we carried out surveillance of La Moneda, the presidential palace, with a view to preparing an armed action. "Propaganda of the deed" was what we had in mind: firing a rocket at the palace.

I staked out the palace for several days. But in the end, the operation, like so many others, was scrubbed because of some conflict among the leadership. Pablo was anxious that I stay involved, but for security reasons he thought I should return to Argentina and maintain the connection between MIR and Cuba from there.

ONE OF MY TRIPS TO HAVANA coincided with the wedding of my younger half-sister. The novelist Gabriel García Márquez was her godfather and, when the wedding was over, he invited me for a drink at his house together with Conchita, my father's old girlfriend, whom he knew well. After spending an enjoyable time with her and García Márquez and other old friends who were there, I got up to say good-bye. Suddenly, some men in uniform arrived and said to us very politely: *"Compañeros,* excuse us, but you may not leave right now because the *comandante* is coming in and we must guarantee his safety."

Shortly afterward, Fidel made his entrance. I was thrilled. I had seen him only once before, with my father when I was still a small boy.

As soon as he walked in, everyone stood up. He greeted us one by one, with an aide making the introductions. It seemed he didn't feel like sitting down, so the meeting took place with everyone standing up. He spoke the whole time, gradually moving from one side of the room to the other, with his fingers interlaced and resting on his chest. For a good fifteen minutes, he spoke about mozzarella cheese—the real kind, *mozzarella bufala*. He was as passionate about the subject as he was about revolution, and said that it would soon be possible to manufacture it in Cuba because he had ordered the buffalos from Naples whose milk was the secret ingredient.

He began next to address individually each one of us who was there. When my turn came, he almost conducted a public interrogation.

"What are you working on?" he asked.

"Journalism," I answered.

"What agency?"

"The newspaper *La Voz.*"

"What section?"

"International."

"I hope that you will be as good as your father," he told me.

When this odd interaction had finished, we were authorized to leave. I got ready to walk out, assuming that Fidel would surely want to speak privately with García Márquez. Fidel shook hands with each of us; when he got to me, he took my arm and separated me from the group.

"Have you met with the Galician?" he asked. It was the friendly nickname they gave Piñeiro. "Because we got a complaint from Alfonsín about the aid we're giving the Chileans via Argentina. Don't worry about it, keep working anyway. But do it right, don't make problems," he told me, smiling.

He obviously wanted me to know that he was aware of what I was doing. His earlier questions had been to put me to the test and to see if I would blurt out some details of the Chilean operation in front of the others.

Upon returning to Buenos Aires I found my mother in the hospital. The doctors told me that her condition was terminal. I decided to take her to Havana, in the hope that there they might find a remedy for her illness. She died three days after our arrival.

I felt that I had lost something that I never had.

12

MANAGUA–PANAMA–CARTAGENA DE INDIAS, 1986

T HE INTERNAL CRISIS OF THE MOVEMENT of the Revolutionary Left (MIR) in Chile soon became open and the members of the organization prepared themselves for factional—possibly fratricidal—struggle. I told Pablo that I'd had enough of this sort of thing in my own country and that if they got their problems sorted out and needed me for operations, they could find me in Cuba.

Piñeiro was on top of the situation within MIR and was not surprised when I told him about Chile. He also agreed that I was right to keep out of the internal struggle. He vexed me, however, because when I tried to tell him my personal problems, including my separation from Silvia, he didn't take my complaints very seriously.

"Well, well . . ." He said. "If you look for another woman, this time don't have any more children, so you won't create any more commitments." And after more censure about my personal life, I finally learned that my next job would be "finding hard currency."

I must confess that at this point my heart really wasn't in it. It appeared to me that the revolutionary movement of Latin America had been completely defeated. Armed struggle was giving way to politics and what little there was left of the movement was dedicating itself to electioneering. But I had no access to this way of life. I was cut out only to be a henchman for someone like Piñeiro: with no family, commitments, country, flag, or religion.

According to Piñeiro, I now had to devote myself to coordinating "missions in search of finances" because "without money you can't make a revolution." For this I would have to move to Nicaragua, obviously a better jumping-off point than Cuba. From there, using my Sandinista ties, I could initiate operational relationships with the various organizations in the Americas. The only thing to guard against, he stipulated, was implicating Cuba in any of these activities.

When I left Piñeiro, I went to the home of Alejandro, who had been my boss in Mexico, to tell him about my new assignment. He had been expelled because of his activities there and punished upon returning home by being made to work in the Central Committee's repair shop for three months. It was a way of taking him out of circulation. He pointed out the moral of his story for me: if things went well, I would have no shortage of patrons in Havana; but if things went wrong or Cuba was implicated in a blown operation, no one would acknowledge me.

Reflecting on these sobering thoughts, I left a few days later for Nicaragua, with money from Piñeiro and a list of names in the Cuban embassies throughout the region in case I needed help.

It was not easy to find a place in Managua, which was still a destination resort for the international revolutionary set. At first, I had to rent a room in a house where several foreigners were living. Among them was a very beautiful Venezuelan woman who possessed three qualities that separately are not annoying, but all together can be aggravating: she was a vegetarian, a feminist and an idiot. On top of everything else, she was called Margarita. Another roommate was a guy called Georgi, who claimed he was a Tamil independence fighter but was actually a very nice hustler who, after having wandered across the world, had somehow wound up in Nicaragua, dancing the salsa and drinking rum like crazy. Last, there was an Italian named Pascualina who worked in the movie theater, I think.

Many of the *compañeros* whom I had to contact were fortunately people I knew from my previous stay in Nicaragua and during the period in which I had worked with the Cuban embassy in Mexico City. For the time being I would not participate in operations, but rather work to link up the various organizations that already had groups trained in this type of work and help them get started. We gave them support and intelligence and arms, as well as finances if they did not already have their own money.

Amid these comings and goings I got to know the representative in Managua of the Colombian revolutionary group M-19.* He was El

---

*M-19 was a non-Marxist-Leninist group descended from the older FARC, which had ties to the Communist Party. Founded in 1974, it got Cuban aid. In the 1980s the organization became notorious for drug running and kidnappings. In 1985 it seized the Palace of Justice in Bogotá and precipitated a blood bath.

Negro Domingo, an excellent *compañero* who had the personable manner typical of Colombians from the Caribbean coast of that country. We became political allies and good friends. It seemed at the time that M-19 was adopting a new style of politics—on the left, yet flexible and free of dogmatism. In Colombia, the movement had substantial political and military visibility. On one occasion, three of its commanders visited Nicaragua: the maximum leader, Carlos Pizarro; "Pedro Pacho," the logistical chief, whose real name was Gerardo Cobo; and Navarro Wolf. The first two were spontaneous and pleasant, but Wolf was arrogant and self-important.

Without spending too much time on politics, we got right down to business. I briefed them on my revolutionary experience, but it was unnecessary to go into detail because they had already received a report on me from El Negro Domingo and other Latin American *compañeros*. Before coming to Nicaragua they had passed through Cuba and Piñeiro had advised them that they should talk with me. Since Pedro Pacho was the chief of logistics, his domain also included finances; so he would have to work with me.

At that point they didn't have any specific objectives. We agreed to meet again in Panama, where they would have more information; and we drew up a communications protocol.

When they left I went back to Havana to see Piñeiro. He was not keen on the idea of operating in Colombia. Although he respected Pizarro's ability in conducting rural guerrilla warfare, he thought that M-19 had committed too many errors in its urban operations. He nevertheless recommended that I continue to nurture the connection. With his advice and more financial support, I left for Panama to meet Pedro Pacho.

Once again the great highways, the shopping centers and the poverty—and the oppressive heat. I made fresh discoveries this time about the Panamanian buses: not only did they have great music playing at full blast—which had already delighted me—but they were each emblazoned with the names of women and their interiors were illuminated with colorful strobe lights. Each bus was like a mobile dancehall.

Once again the cheap little hotel, the hours of walking around to make sure I was not being followed. The meeting was at the Don Lee on Fiftieth Street, an Americanized Chinese restaurant. When somebody approached me and asked, "Are you Steven's friend?" I was supposed to answer: "No, his cousin." My contact would be carrying a copy of *Life* magazine.

The appointment was set for 8:30. Fifteen minutes went by and no one showed up. Just as I was about to leave, a taxi drew up and a Colombian-looking young man hurriedly got out. He wasn't carrying anything in his hand. He came up to me and asked: "Are you Martín?" Seeing my surprise, he added, smiling: "Sorry, but I forgot the password. I'm Geronimo and I work with Pedro Pacho." So much for the protocols of clandestine operations.

After exchanging small talk with me, he said that we had to go because Pedro Pacho was waiting for us in the office. I was surprised that a secret organization like M-19 would have an office in a foreign country. But I went with him. The taxi dropped us off in front of one of the most sordid bars I have ever seen in my life. This was the office. They called it "Come on, Come on" because, Geronimo told me laughing, "We always say, come on, come on, let's go have a meeting!"

Sitting there among the pimps and prostitutes was Pedro Pacho. He was with his wife, called La Negra, and another *compañero* who went by the nickname Sardine. Since it was not the most appropriate place to discuss the missions we were contemplating, we made an appointment for the next day to go somewhere quieter.

On that occasion Pedro Pacho came personally. He told me they were planning the kidnapping of an American businessman who worked for Texaco and lived in Barranquilla, Colombia. The job did not seem difficult, because government repression was less severe on the Caribbean coast. They would be in charge of the intelligence work and the kidnapping itself, while I and other Latin American colleagues would manage the hostage's detention and picking up the ransom; and yet another group of Colombians would be in charge of the negotiations. We decided that I would travel to Havana to organize their getaway from Panama.

Back in Havana, I spoke again with Piñeiro. He thought the target was fine, but he was bothered because I couldn't give him more specifics about the American: his name, his job, etc. I told him I would learn more. We decided that in the first phase, a single *compañero* would travel with me to Barranquilla and, once we were installed and in liaison with M-19, two other *compañeros* would join us. Piñeiro would pick up the tab for our travel and the money needed to set us up in Colombia. M-19 would cover the cost of maintaining us in Colombia for as long as the job took.

When I returned to Panama, Pedro Pacho was already back from his trip to Colombia. He decided that it would be best to gather in Cartagena de Indias because it was a very touristy place and no one would pay much attention to the presence of foreigners. We were to meet in the coffee shop of the Hotel Don Blas. Since Pedro didn't know that I would be back so soon from Havana, he had already set the meeting for twenty days later. We decided to remain in Panama waiting for the date to approach. Almost every day I met with Sardine and Pedro Pacho.

Pedro was totally unlike the revolutionary leaders I had known up till then. His political career had begun in the Bolivian ELN, from which he was expelled because, as he told me laughing, they caught him masturbating in a guerrilla camp. Before that he had been a journalist; so had his girlfriend, La Negra, who used to be on Colombian television. Having endured the traditional left's dogmatic view of the world, he not only seemed very flexible with regard to politics, but also easygoing about the foibles of his subordinates. Very knowledgeable about the popular culture of his country, he possessed a surprisingly artistic sensibility.

Finally the day came to leave for Colombia. My friend Luis of the Chilean MIR came with me. We took the same flight, but didn't sit together or give any sign that we knew each other, as a basic precautionary measure so that one of us would not be compromised if the other had problems at customs with his false documents. After landing at Cartagena we joined up outside the airport as if we were tourists who happened to have agreed to take the same taxi downtown and split the fare.

For three days we waited for the tie-up with M-19. The contact arrived on the fourth day. This one scrupulously maintained the agreed-upon passwords. He was young and full of enthusiasm. He brought with him more good will than information, which worried me a little and made me wonder if the Colombians underestimated the preparation required for such a job. They had personal and professional information about our target, but they were not familiar with his routine activities and movements. They knew he traveled with bodyguards but they didn't know how many or what type of weapons they used. In other words, there was a lot left to do. Though it wasn't our responsibility, Luis and I decided to help them get the logistics cleared up.

After two months we finally had the necessary information. All that was left was to put the finishing touches on the plan. But at that moment, Texaco's management asked our target to return to the United States and sent a new executive to replace him. That meant we had to start again almost from scratch. We decided to leave

Colombia, where things were hot, and not come back again until the Colombians advised us they were ready.

I was back in Nicaragua when I heard that Pedro Pacho had been arrested with La Negra. Shortly afterward their bodies were found in a village in the interior of Colombia—hers with broken bones; his riddled with bullets; both with clear signs of having been brutally tortured.

Their deaths complicated things, because Pedro was fully informed about the operation and had obviously been alive for some time in the hands of the Colombian security agencies before being executed. But as time passed with still no roundup, we came to believe that he hadn't talked and we decided to go forward. Our bad luck continued, however. One of the members of the group charged with gathering information was also arrested. At that point we decided to suspend the operation. Too many errors had already been committed and there were too many security problems.

BACK IN MANAGUA, I RAN INTO ONE of my old *compañeros* from Argentina whom I liked and respected. He seemed burned out physically and unhappy. We had a few drinks together. At first he was a little tense, but soon he relaxed and began to tell me how he had remained in Managua with Pelado Gorriarán's group, with which he had participated in some operations on behalf of Nicaraguan intelligence. But then, political differences had arisen. He was allowed to resign from the organization, but he had been compromised by the operations in which he had participated. Pelado withheld his documents and convinced the Nicaraguans not to let him leave Managua—he was practically a prisoner. His wife and children were in Buenos Aires; he had no contact with them and was not allowed to write home.

The situation seemed the more absurd since he was an absolutely trustworthy individual. The fact that he might go to visit his family in Argentina did not entail that he would betray any secrets. In the past he had participated in many important efforts and never had there been the slightest problem. He had been jailed in Argentina and had not talked even under torture.

I spent the next day checking into the case. The Nicaraguans couldn't tell me anything and I understood that for them it was an internal problem for Pelado Gorriarán's people. So I went to see one of the few *compañeros* working for Pelado with whom I was still friends.

I casually asked him, as if it were no big deal to me, about the guerrilla in question. After some evasions he answered: "He's crazy—he's been hitting the bottle lately. Besides, he's a broken man."

Acting innocent, I asked why they didn't just send him to Argentina; after all, he was over fifty years old and in poor health; he had gone through a lot and it was better that he should be with his family. His answer explained everything.

"I think so too, but Pelado is convinced that once he's back in Argentina he'll get into politics. If he sets up there and people find out he's not with Pelado any longer, some *compañeros,* taking into account his career and prestige, might become demoralized and follow his cause."

The man wasn't broken. Nor was he going to give information to the enemy. His problem was that he did not agree politically with Pelado. It was painful for me to understand all this. I still had a measure of affection for Pelado despite my political differences with him, but clearly he was no longer the same man I had felt proud to work with. When he returned to Managua after the assassination of Somoza, the Sandinistas had rewarded him with the rank of major. Little by little he ceased to be Pelado and turned into "Comandante Ricardo." Like the other *comandantes,* he lived in a luxurious house in Managua and was chauffered around in a Mercedes Benz. He insisted on being the unique voice of our old organization. There were even rumors that he went so far as to kill Argentine militants who dared criticize him.

I was in a difficult situation. I could either do something for this man, embroiling myself in problems that did not directly concern me, or I could keep my mouth shut. I opted for the first course. I knew that if I took the case to the Nicaraguans or to the Cubans they would be in agreement with Pelado, so it was better to act on my own. I talked to the *compañero* and suggested that we organize his escape from Managua.

It wasn't complicated. I began by asking the Salvadoran guerrillas to falsify an example of a Honduran passport someone had given me. Not lying to them, I simply told them it was for a *compañero* who worked with me. Passport in hand, all I had to do was wait for Martín, the Cuban official who "ran" me in Managua, to go to Havana. Fortunately we did not have to wait long. The day after Martín left for Havana, my friend and I flew to Mexico City. I helped him buy his ticket for Argentina and watched him board a plane to return to his family. For me, this was the end of the matter, but not for the Nicaraguans or for Pelado, who would later use it against me.

I WAS ALWAYS ON THE GO during this period, shuttling between various countries in Central America. One time in Panama I met up with a *compañero* who had been the M-19 representative in Havana. He told me that his movement was going to hold a military conference in the Colombian countryside. Pizarro, the organization's commander whom I had known in Managua, wanted me to come so we could resume the operational relationship that had been cut off by the brutal death of Pedro Pacho—setting up an American businessman for kidnap.

I asked him to grant me a day to make up my mind. Actually, I had to check with the Cubans. The contact arrangements were, fortunately, fast and easy. The procedure was to call the Cuban embassy in Panama from a pay phone, using the ridiculous pseudonym of Aramís, and chat about trivialities with someone from the Americas Department. This was a signal for a meeting at the same time on the following day at a previously agreed-on spot.

A man named Cabrerita came the next day. I cannot recall what I told him in order to convince him how urgently I needed to travel to Colombia, but it worked; he sent a message to Piñeiro and the response came quickly back: there were no objections. That same afternoon I went to see the M-19 *compañero* to inform him that I was at his disposal. He told me that we'd leave by boat the next day.

Around two in the afternoon he came to get me and took me to a house in Panama City. There we waited until ten o'clock at night before leaving for Isla Grande, near Porto Belo at the northern end of the country. Once there, we checked into an inn to rest for what remained of the night. Early next day, we embarked for Colombia. I couldn't believe my eyes when I saw the boat they had been boasting to me about. It was barely nine feet long and had an outboard motor. The sea was pretty rough, but five of us clambered aboard. I am compelled to admit that my throat was dry and my hands had fastened a death grip on the bench I was sitting on. But once under way, there was no turning back.

The captain, fortunately, acted like someone who knew what he was doing. This awareness helped to calm my nerves, though I was forced to endure more than one moment in which I was convinced the sea would be my tomb. The tormenting travel experience lasted a full day and a half. As night approached we took shelter on a tiny island, resuming our voyage at first light. We came ashore in Colombia at midday, at a spot on the Atlantic coast named Capurganá.

We had gotten there without having to pass through any checkpoint!

This place, ravishingly beautiful, was luxuriant with tropical vegetation and sported a little beach. The only tourists were Colombians. We checked into a comfortable little wooden inn where some *compañeros* were expecting us. Some would continue the trip by sea, and others, I among them, would fly.

The next day, with a *compañero* whom we called Nicolás, we left for Medellín. There we hooked up with a female M-19 contact who took us to Calí by car. We got there on December 24. That night, along with *compañeros* we met there, we went to a working-class barrio to celebrate Christmas Eve; everyone who lived there was aware that some people from M-19 were present, but they reassured us that we were safe with them.

Two days later we left by car. After passing through endless sugar-cane fields on a long drive, we stopped at a farm worker's house. We met other *compañeros* there and were given rubber boots, backpacks, blankets, tarps and eating utensils. Thus equipped, we started hiking toward the central mountain range. There were seven of us, including two women, one of whom was the strongest walker in the group.

As we drew closer to our destination, we encountered bands of armed *compañeros*. They greeted us warmly and guided us along the mountain trails. We arrived safely at the camp on December 31.

The camp held some sixty fighters, Carlos Pizarro among them. I didn't see him right away because he was busy making preparations for the meeting, but I did have the pleasure of seeing Andrés, a youthful *compañero* with whom I had fought in Nicaragua. We stared at each other for a moment, each of us looking for a sign of recognition, before we embraced. It was perfectly normal for him to be there because he was in M-19, but my presence must have come as a total shock.

We stepped aside to talk about things. After the war in Nicaragua, he had gone to Cuba for further military training. Then he had traveled to Panama in order to set off for Colombia along with a group of *compañeros*. He told me that upon arriving in Colombia they had fallen into the hands of the Colombian military. They were released after a year in prison. Then he hooked up with M-19 in Medellín and was appointed one of their leaders. He had come to the meeting so he could confer with Pizarro.

Toward six in the evening, farm workers and people from the nearby villages started to show up. Some fighters from FARC, the older guerrilla army, arrived as well. After a short speech by Pizarro, the party got under way. The *compañeros*, rifles on their shoulders, danced with local girls wearing their traditional outfits. And there was *sancocho*, and *chicha* and *aguardiente.** The festivities were guarded, of course, by guerrillas stationed nearby.

On the following day, with the *guayabo*—Colombian slang for a hangover—that I'd been suffering more or less continuously since Christmas Eve, I got together with Pizarro. This time everything was brought out into the open: the Nicaraguans' lack of solidarity with the Colombian fighters; what it was like dealing with the Cubans; and, above all, what had happened to Pedro Pacho. Pizarro thought that Pedro had gotten far too careless, not out of a spirit of negligence but because he'd been demanding far too much of himself. His death had been a terrible blow to the organization. And Pizarro told me that the point of the conference was to develop a political strategy for the entire movement. Being organized into rural, urban and international fronts, without much coordination—at some points, none at all—meant that M-19 lacked an overall political outlook. Comrades from the different fronts had been brought together to discuss what goals to pursue. Pizarro knew it wouldn't be easy, but he trusted in his activists' spirit of unity.

In the afternoon, we organized ourselves to head out toward the campground where we'd be holding the meeting. I arranged to fall into Andrés' squad. Each group was made up of seven men and women. Because so many people had come in from the city, there weren't weapons enough to go around. Each group got two. I ended up with a G-3 rifle; it weighed a ton and was missing the screw for the front grip, which was attached by a piece of wire.

The going was easy for the first night, thanks to level ground. And we even went some of the way by truck. The hard part came the next day when we headed up into the hills. I was having a problem with my knees, a result of the soft city life I'd gotten used to, my failure to keep fit and difficulties adjusting to the altitude. I felt utterly worthless. For the five days we were on the march, I got silicone injections in my knees to ease the pain. But that solved only part of my problem. Between my exhaustion and the altitude sickness, I thought I might not make it. On top of that, in the highlands, at more than 12,000 feet, we were constantly going from cold to hot weather with no transition. If I bundled up, the hiking would get me sweating, so I would take my jacket off and almost die of cold as my sweat suddenly seemed to freeze. My knapsack, and the G-3, which I'd been

---

Sancocho is a stew made with fish or chicken, plantain and cassava. *Chica* is an alcoholic drink made from fermented corn. *Aguardiente* is a very potent fruit juice brandy.

pestering everyone to be given, became such burdens that I couldn't wait to get rid of them.

At night we would sleep in pairs, as close together as possible to fight off the cold. Fortunately, at that altitude, there's a plant that Colombians call *frailejón* and if you put enough down for a sort of mattress, it conserves and transmits body heat. How I loved *frailejón!*

On January 6, we finally made it to the main campsite. There we found other Colombians who had made preparations for our arrival. There were about seventy of them and they were waiting with a real feast: lentils and *changarinas,* a fried chip made of flour.

Next day, after the morning assembly, we settled down to a meeting. There were many things to discuss, but they all centered on the criteria for alliances and the nature of armed struggle. Given the number of different positions that were represented, any other Latin American left-wing organization would have split wide open. At first, I have to say, I felt that such a result was inevitable for us too. But as the days passed, the way people expressed themselves made me think that M-19 had hit on a new way of settling differences, a much more democratic approach than in any of the other groups I had been associated with.

After a week of these discussions, working groups were appointed to come up with proposals to be put before a plenary assembly. I asked Pizarro if I could join the group on urban operations, which was what I knew best. But I did not have much familiarity with the general situation in Colombia, so I made only minor contributions, deferring to more experienced comrades. But their laid-back attitude toward internal security concerned me, as did their eagerness to go into action without worrying much about casualties.

The future would show that my concerns were well founded. Of the five *compañeros* that made up this working group, at least three are dead. I've had no news of the others.

Finally, Pizarro met with some comrades individually to coordinate some operational issues. He asked me to help in two specific areas. One concerned a store of rifles and RPG-7 bazookas they had assembled in Nicaragua. The quantity was modest, but, as I had seen for myself, they badly needed weapons. Given their bad relations with the Nicaraguans, they figured they would have a hard time getting them to release the hardware. The Sandinistas maintained that the Nicaraguan Revolution was a reality that had to be preserved, whereas the revolutionary projects in other countries were fantasies. I would have to do whatever it took to organize the shipment without the Nicas finding out.

The other request was to resume the financing work we had tried to initiate with Pedro Pacho because the money situation was deteriorating.

The first mission seemed relatively easy.

The second one, necessarily involving kidnappings and expropriations, looked to be more complicated. After my experience in Cartagena, there was no way I could deal with M-19 in that kind of work unless I had absolute independence of action, relying on them only for weapons, and for help in the event of security problems. We came to an agreement and Pizarro introduced me to a *compañero* named Pedro from Medellín who could help me out in that sort of situation.

We pulled out of the zone in small groups, which then subdivided again so that we came into Calí two by two. I came with Pedro. He proposed that we continue together to Medellín, but I had to go through Bogotá first, where I had an appointment with some Colombians I had known in Panama who had set up a counterfeiting operation. This opened up another possibility for liberating funds for revolutionary organizations, and one that was less risky than bank jobs. Pedro and I planned to hook up again later.

The day I arrived in Bogotá, my contact told me that they had been able to forge dollars of excellent quality, except they were having trouble getting the correct texture on the paper. Then they used a chemical process to wash out a legitimate one-dollar bill and reprint it as a fifty- or hundred-dollar bill, so they needed a lot of one-dollar bills.

Because U.S. dollars are the only currency that circulates in Panama, the simplest plan seemed to be to obtain them there and smuggle them into Colombia. The Colombians said they'd give me 50 percent of the take in return for putting up the first $10,000 to be altered. I said that I wanted to see a sample, and we arranged to meet the same night.

I couldn't believe what I saw. The altered hundred-dollar bills were amazing. I was no expert, but for the ordinary man on the street there was no way to tell the counterfeit bills from the real thing. I took the samples and said I had to meet with my superiors, the counterfeiters and I arranging to meet in Panama sixty days later. If the response of my superiors was positive, I would return armed with a specific plan for carrying out the operation.

I took the first flight to Nicaragua and met with Navarro Wolf. I laid out the details of the conference in Colombia and the weapons operation that Pizarro had asked me to supervise. Navarro flatly opposed it, arguing there was no money to carry it off. I said I would figure out a way to get it. Then he confessed that that wasn't the only problem. He was also worried about compromising our relations with the Sandinista Front. Even my arguments about the urgent needs of the fighters in the mountains of Colombia couldn't budge him.

I came away from the meeting in an angry mood. Bad luck seemed to be pursuing me. I got the idea of asking one of the *compañeros* in the house where I was staying to lend me his motorcycle, because I didn't have a car and public transportation under the Sandinistas was awful. I hadn't gone half a kilometer when I skidded on sand while taking a curve: I was going too fast and lost control. The accident wasn't as serious as it might have been, but my foot was fractured in several places. So, with a cast and crutches, and in an even fouler mood, I took off for Havana.

When Piñeiro saw me he asked what had happened. I told him, and he said only: "You're acting like a jerk."

Then we got onto the subject of the counterfeit dollars. I showed him the samples. He said he'd think it over and let me know soon.

Two days later I was in his office again. At first I thought he would say no. He started off saying that passing counterfeit currency was a very difficult job—that when these dollars showed up in the market, the Americans would try to trace their origin, and if Cuba were seen to be involved, one way or the other, the repercussions were easy to foresee. Then his tone changed.

"Of course, if the operation is put together the right way, we won't have to show up in it. And if we run off a big batch and wait a while before doing another, it will be difficult for them to discover the source. . . ."

He finished by saying that he would back me if I would take responsibility for any problems that developed. For his part, he would take it upon himself to recruit some Latin American organization that would be a cover in case of complications. On the spot he passed over an envelope with the first $10,000 and told me not to worry. They had friends in Panama and circulating the bills would be easy. All I had to do was get the real one-dollar bills to Colombia and the fake hundred-dollar bills back to Panama.

I rented a boat to take me to Puerto Obaldia on the Colombian border. Halfway there, the boat took on water and my cast got soaked. I had to remove it when I got to Puerto Obaldía, and bought a bandage and an elastic stocking to replace it. Then I flew to Paitilla, the airport in Panama City. I found that the luggage of passengers coming from the Colombian border got a thorough going-over; that meant the route was all right to get the bills to Colombia, but not to bring them back. I stayed a month in Panama looking for other solutions to the problem. Through a contact who let us use his name, I opened a bank account to deposit the $10,000. To turn it into one-dollar bills, we would have to open a cover business allowing us to get small-denomination change. I headed back to Havana to tell Piñeiro. By this time, my foot was so swollen that I couldn't stand on it.

The steps I had taken met with Piñeiro's approval. All he asked was that I check with the counterfeiters to see if they could make Japanese yen and German marks instead of dollars because they were easier to pass. When we said goodbye he noticed my crutches and was surprised that I was still suffering the aftereffects of the motor-cycle crash. He told me I couldn't leave Cuba before seeing an ortho-pedist. I tried to argue, but it was no use—I would need a doctor's authorization to go back to work.

13

HAVANA, 1988

WHEN I WENT TO SEE THE DOCTOR, I learned that the problem was much more serious than I had thought. Not only had the bone fused badly, but I also had an advanced case of osteoporosis, a rare disease for a person of my age, though the doctor told me it could also occur as a result of great stress. He said that if it couldn't be controlled through physical therapy, he might have to amputate my leg to prevent the osteoporosis from spreading to the knee.

For the first time in my life I was truly disciplined. I religiously attended every session of physical therapy even though, deep inside, I was convinced that my leg was already lost. Soon I noticed a certain improvement, but my tendency toward self-pity and self-dramatization went out of control.

Like the condemned man whose days are numbered, I tried to enjoy everything life has to offer. I was sure that if I lost my leg, no woman would look at me, so I made a point of trying to seduce every woman who crossed my path, regardless of age or looks. Sometimes my efforts succeeded; usually they failed. But my perseverance was such that I always could count on having someone to go out with. Never had I devoted myself so obsessively to promiscuity.

My recovery took almost five months and my leg was saved. But in the meantime my stock with the Cubans had fallen. It was not just that I had been out of circulation. Several of my irregular activities during my stay in Nicaragua had come to the attention of the Sandinistas, who complained to the Cubans. In addition, Navarro Wolf, a member of the high command of M-19, on one of his trips to Havana had come to visit me during my convalescence. I was still smarting over his refusal to support the shipment of RPG-2 grenade launchers that Pizarro had asked for. We began to argue and almost came to blows. I never spoke further about this, but he immediately went to Piñeiro. They also held it against me that I had helped smuggle the Argentine *compañero* out of Nicaragua, where Gorriarán was keeping him as a virtual prisoner. Finally—and this was in all probability the most serious problem, or at least that's what I thought—I had expressed some hesitant criticisms of the Cuban regime and some of its leaders, and this was forbidden.

Thus, I found myself once again without work and without prospects. Of course I had no financial problems because I received a monthly stipend from the Americas Department. It was a kind of pension, and indeed I felt almost retired at the age of thirty-three. I spent my time visiting Latin American comrades whom I had known during my activities. Nostalgia was a common illness among us all. Inevitably our conversations turned to the problem of why our revolutionary guerrilla projects had been defeated.

The retelling of old anecdotes forced us to admit that almost all our friends were dead and we were the survivors of a history we still did not understand. Yet to admit defeat would mean abandoning our dead.

What was to be done?

It was evident that armed struggle was a blind alley. Without the support of the people, it had become a Mafia activity. But however apparent this was, it was also true that armed struggle had an almost scriptural power over the revolutionary mind. For us, it was an enigma.

ONE DAY WHEN I WAS AT CONCHITA'S HOUSE, she asked me to accompany her to the office of Tony de la Guardia. I was excited. I had met Tony during the war in Nicaragua and run into him several times in Havana as well. We were not yet what you would call friends, but to me he seemed very likable. He smiled easily and had a sharp sense of humor. We arrived at his office in the residential neighborhood of Siboney, and he received us cordially. He was wearing an olive-drab uniform with a colonel's stripes. He kept the U.S.-made M-16 rifle he had used while fighting in Nicaragua behind his desk, along with many photographs from his time in that country. There were also other weapons that he had used on other missions.

"So, Conchita, now you're going around with a terrorist for an escort, eh?" Tony joked.

After talking with her, he turned to me and asked how I was and what I was doing. I tried to explain my confused situation to him. I told him I could return to Argentina but didn't know what I would do there. Or I might go to El Salvador, where the guerrilla campaign of the FMLN was underway. Or maybe leave to fight with M-19 in Colombia if I could make contact with Pizarro without having to go through Navarro. Tony listened patiently. As we parted he told me that I should come back the next day; he might have something to offer me.

I was back in his office the next morning. The prospect of working with someone of his stature was exciting. So many stories were told about him that it was difficult to determine where reality ended and legend began. I knew that he had been sent to Lebanon during the war with the Israelis, to Chile in the days of Salvador Allende's government, and to Nicaragua for the final offensive. He had organized the military training of numerous guerrilla groups in different countries of Latin America. I was aware that he used to direct a group that was part of the Cuban General Intelligence Agency (DGI), which carried out important secret missions for the Cuban Revolution and, directly, for Fidel.

When he arrived, he was surprised to see me waiting for him. He offered me coffee and we chatted casually while sitting on his sofa. In broad outline he explained to me that the organization he now led was in charge of breaking the U.S. trade embargo and obtaining technology for various branches of industry and medicine. Only the North Americans possessed such products, and because of the embargo, Cuba could not buy them legally and was forced to acquire them through illegal mechanisms.

He was charged, in addition, to pursue foreign currency by all possible means, legal or illegal, because Cuba lacked the necessary funds to buy supplies for its various ministries. The name of the special section that Tony led inside the DGI was called MC, which was simply the initials for *moneda convertible,* or "convertible currency."

He continued telling me why Fidel had granted him a sort of "letter of marque" in the manner of the corsairs of old—a fact that Fidel himself would later confirm in an interview with the Italian journalist Gianni Mina when he said:

> MC arose as an activity against the blockade.... I have already told you that everything we might do against the blockade is legitimate, because we consider it immoral and unjust that a powerful country, the greatest economic power in the world, should try to blockade a country like Cuba, which is struggling for its welfare and for its development. And therefore I tell you that everything we might do against the blockade we considered legitimate, we considered it moral. These people had the mission of breaking the blockade, even

if it was only symbolically in some cases, even if it did not solve substantial problems: the United States did not want to import Cuban articles. They did not want us to export tobacco and [MC allowed us] to export tobacco in small quantities. It was almost a symbolic thing. They didn't want us to export rum, yet we used to export rum. But above all if they did not want us to get a certain piece of computer equipment, we would go and look for that computer. If they did not want us to have spare parts for industries or for certain machines of North American origin, we would use clandestine methods to buy spare parts in the United States and bring them to Cuba. That was the kind of service that MC fundamentally rendered, and it served various state agencies because all the agencies needed something.... How did they do that? They would organize certain enterprises: this enterprise, that enterprise, or an enterprise in one place and an enterprise in another. In other words, they had a kind of letter of marque, let's say.

Cuba's needs kept growing, especially when perestroika caused Soviet aid to decline. To meet his objectives, Tony had set up several commercial businesses for MC. They were legal, but were registered under Panamanian or other nationalities; they were able to play in the capitalist market and at the same time provide cover for other, embargo-avoiding activities. One of these companies was Merbar, which was devoted to imports and exports through Panama. It would buy merchandise for resale in shops for foreigners in Cuba—chiefly consumer electronics—and in Africa—clothing or information equipment. This was the enterprise Tony suggested I represent in Angola. He already knew about the coming withdrawal of Cuban troops from Africa, and he thought it important that some people remain there as "sleeper" agents who didn't have obvious Cuban connections. As an Argentine, I fit the bill. Given my absolute ignorance about commercial questions, he suggested that I should work for a while in his Havana offices to familiarize myself with the vocabulary.

The truth is that the prospect of an overnight metamorphosis into a businessman did not excite me in the least. But I accepted Tony's offer in the hope that at some later point he would move me back into the field of covert activities.

AS WE BEGAN WORKING TOGETHER, my admiration for Tony grew. I was taken by his mythic reputation as a revolutionary hero, of course, but

I also admired him because of his capacity for friendship and the way he took care of colleagues and subordinates.

This regard carried me along despite the work I was doing. Especially at the beginning, learning the basic concepts of business was deadly boring and had nothing to do with what I had done until then. Imagine: a revolutionary studying to be a capitalist!

Nevertheless, it had the advantage of being a stable job and it gave a certain structure to my personal life, which had of late been a disaster. That also began to change one Saturday afternoon when I was in the house of my half-sister Laura and a friend came to visit me. My friend was accompanied by a girl with very fine skin and a sweet way about her; I was charmed the minute I saw her. I had actually spotted her on the beach some months before, but never thought I would meet her.

It was just like being struck by the proverbial lightning. She instantly became the focus of my being for the next five minutes, for the coming years, forever. When my friend and the wonderful young woman got up to leave, I offered to go with them without even knowing where they were headed; it could have been to the end of the world for all I cared. Luckily, they weren't going that far, just to the home of the grandparents of the woman who, from then on, would be my constant companion. I sensed that she was not indifferent to me, and this encouraged me. I couldn't stop talking as we walked.

"What's your name?"

"Ileana."

"Where do you work?"

"I'm a psychologist."

"Where do you live?"

"In Miramar."

For my part, I don't even remember how many lies I told.

Her profession disappointed me; all my instincts told me that relationships with women in that line of work were dangerous. I could tell that my friend was nervous about all the attention I was focusing on Ileana.

We got to the home of Ileana's grandparents. My friend managed to take me aside: "You're crazy. Don't you know who she is?"

I said, "No, but I love her."

"What? You don't know that she's your boss's daughter?"

I was surprised that I had never seen her in Tony's office and that she was so humble. The children of high officials in Cuba usually behave like a caste apart, flaunting their dynastic privileges. But Ileana was different. This made sense, since Tony himself was different. He had no interest in posturing as part of the ruling class of the Revolution. I would discover later that the whole family was the same way.

We stayed a few minutes at Ileana's grandparents' house, enough time for me to ask for her telephone number. It was not the same as Tony's because her parents had divorced a long time before and she lived with her mother. That same night I called to ask her out. To my great joy, she told me to come by her house. I quickly showered and changed clothes. Thus I also met Lucila, Ileana's mother, a very nice woman but one who happened at that moment to stand in the way of my plans of seduction. I had barely begun talking with Ileana when she came to sit with us and offered me an herbal tea. Upon learning that I was Argentine, she asked if I knew Daniel Hopen, a fellow member of the ERP who had disappeared.

Of course I knew him! Daniel—"Ariel"—was one of the first comrades I met when I joined the organization. Lucila told me that during his long stay in Cuba—this was after her divorce from Tony—Daniel was her boyfriend, a relationship that was interrupted when he had to return to Argentina. Our shared memories of Daniel and the fact that I told Lucila she had the most beautiful eyes in Havana, which was not far from the truth, enabled me to win her over. Ever since, we have had a good relationship.

After several hours of nostalgic discussion, Lucila finally left us alone. Ileana and I continued talking until four in the morning. At that hour, it was clear we had either to say goodbye or sleep together. We opted for the second alternative. From that moment on we have never been separated.

A week later, Tony called me into his office. I had preferred not to say anything about Ileana because I was afraid it might impede my work in Angola. But he had already checked around to see if I had a girlfriend. Because of the type of work I would be doing in Angola and the extended time I would have to stay there, perhaps as much as five years, he favored *compañeros* who had wives. This is how he found out I was with his daughter.

What he didn't know was that we were already living together and that not long after we met, on a day of craziness, I had proposed to Ileana that she come to Angola with me. Since she is even crazier than I am, she answered yes.

Tony told me that the next day I would accompany him to Angola. He had some work to do there and to him it seemed a good idea that I should come along in order to become more familiar with the place and with the members of the organization there. He took me by surprise when he added: "Next time you go with Ileana."

He had already spoken with his daughter before seeing me.

It was one of the most exhausting flights I have ever taken—almost sixteen hours, with a stopover of one hour in Cape Verde. It was a military plane, so full of soldiers that you couldn't even stretch your legs. All of them were going to Angola as representatives of Fidel's "internationalism."

We landed in Luanda at dawn. Tony's twin brother, Brigadier-General Patricio de la Guardia, was waiting at the airport for us. He was chief of the Cuban Ministry of the Interior's mission in Angola. If Patricio had not been wearing a uniform and Tony civilian clothes, I would not have been able to tell them apart. We took a pickup truck to the Ministry of the Interior's headquarters, located next to the embassy. Patricio, laughing, told us that on one of his last trips to the south of the country, the airplane had crashed on takeoff and he had been almost killed. He had flirted with danger since the days of the Revolution and had been everywhere, including Vietnam, where he had served in combat against the U.S. troops. Since then he had been head of the Ministry of the Interior, chief of staff of the Special Troops, and leader of the Cuban delegation in Michael Manley's Jamaica.

TONY AND I SET UP SHOP in Patricio's apartment building. They gave me a room on the floor where the *compañeros* of the MC Department resided. My only responsibilities were going with Tony to his work meetings and getting to know Luanda.

The misery was extraordinary. There was no running water; people got their water from dirty streams. The children suffered from rickets.

One day I witnessed a scene that both surprised and confused me. I was driving along with a friend from the Cuban Special Troops whom I had met in Havana. In a very humble village—Angolans call them *quimbe*—soldiers from the Angolan army were herding men into a truck, beating them with their rifle butts. I asked if this was an operation against UNITA, the "counterrevolutionary enemy" backed by the United States. Lowering his head, my friend told me: "No, it's forced recruitment by the army. I don't know what the hell we're doing here."

Soon I was asking myself the same question. I knew that Patricio had personally told Fidel that the Cuban forces were an army of occupation in Angola and that the problems there were ethnic, not political.

The night before our return to Havana we ate dinner with other *compañeros* from MC at Patricio's house. General Arnoldo Ochoa, the chief of the military mission in Angola and the most powerful military figure in Cuba, was present. I was somewhat intimidated, but his simplicity and his sense of humor surprised me. His manner was that of a typical Cuban from the countryside. Ochoa had been introduced to combat as a very young man in the Sierra Maestra, under the command of Camilo Cienfuegos, one of the heroes of the Cuban Revolution. Together with Cienfuegos, he participated in the invasion from the eastern end of the island to the west and in the battle that crowned Fidel Castro's triumph in January 1959. He had been trained as a career officer in the USSR. Later he joined the Venezuelan guerrilla movement and led the Cuban contingent there. Then he led Cuban forces in Angola, Eritrea and, most famously, Ethiopia, where he directed a joint Soviet-Cuban force against the Somalian army. He had also advised the Sandinistas in the war against the Contras. Finally, as chief of the Cuban forces in Angola, he had compelled the South Africans to sit at the negotiating table after having inflicted heavy defeats on their proxy forces. He had been awarded the Order of National Heroes of Cuba, the highest honor a Cuban can receive.

Ochoa was like any other comrade, telling jokes or yarning about his amorous conquests; that first impression of the common soldier stayed with me.

Tony continued on to Europe and I returned to Havana. Ileana was waiting for me. We stayed two days at her mother's house before moving into my apartment. It was not very comfortable, but we needed our own space. Our furniture consisted of one mattress, a refrigerator and a Vietnamese wicker table; but we were together.

Once again, my happiness was interrupted by something that happened in other latitudes. On January 23, 1989, a group of guerrillas attacked the army barracks at La Tablada, in a suburb of Buenos Aires. After the smoke cleared, twenty guerrillas were dead. When I first heard it, the news seemed impossible. At that time the political situation in Argentina was unstable: there were constant rumors of a military coup. But democracy still prevailed, and it was insane to begin guerrilla action at such a moment. I even considered the possibility that it might be a provocation by the military's extreme faction.

That night, I got a call summoning me to a meeting with Piñeiro. I found him more tense and nervous than I had ever seen him. He told me: "They should build a monument to Pelado made of shit."

I understood that he was referring to my old comrade and

nemesis Pelado Gorriarán. So it had been he and his group who attacked the barracks. That famous maxim immediately came to mind: success has a thousand fathers, but failure is an orphan. Only recently I had been talking with Piñeiro about Gorriarán's political program in Argentina and he hadn't been able to praise him enough. When I warned him of Pelado's militaristic tendencies, Piñeiro dismissed my comments as arising from some personal vendetta.

I was deeply disturbed by the deaths of these fighters. With the Americas Department official in charge of Argentina I reviewed the news reports and videos of the massacre they had recorded off television. The combat had lasted more than sixteen hours. The cruelty and ruthlessness of the Argentine military was evident. You could see in the videos how they shot *compañeros* who had dropped their weapons and were surrendering with their hands on the backs of their necks. They wanted no prisoners.

I was even more distraught when I saw the list of the dead: most of them were my friends. I had shared the same dreams, the same risks, the same joys, the same sorrows with them. Fat Man Sanchez, with whom I had fought in Nicaragua, was there; Caldú, the Little Galician, always smiling, chasing some skirt in Mexico or Managua or wherever he was; Sugar Cane, always talking about weapons and combat; and so many others—stupidly sent to their deaths in a senseless operation that none of the Argentine people they had claimed to be serving would have approved.

Pelado had gotten out alive. Some say he participated in the actual fighting, others that he directed it from elsewhere. What is certain, in my opinion, is that he has on his conscience, if he still has one, the immense burden of having senselessly sent so many young revolutionaries to their deaths.

The surprising thing about the reports was that among the dead and arrested were not only seasoned militants of the ERP, but also very young boys from the lower-class neighborhoods of Buenos Aires. The former fought perhaps out of nostalgia, because they were unable to accept defeat and because they couldn't face the prolonged political struggle that democracy requires. But these youngsters—why did they fight and die?

This tragedy profoundly affected me: it was the end of an era. And the final bitter irony was that my dead *compañeros* had given the military, who had been staging coups, assassinations and "disappearances" for forty years, an opportunity to play the role of defenders of democracy.

A FEW WEEKS LATER, PATRICIO WAS IN Havana on leave. The day he arrived we had dinner with him. That was when he started to call me "Terrorist." We talked about everything—above all, about mutual friends who, as usual, were dead or in jail. I noticed that when I tried to talk to him about Angola, however, he avoided the subject; he would only say tersely that he was delighted Ileana and I were going there. We quickly became inseparable. Sometimes we tried to avoid going to his house so he could meet with other friends; but then he would come looking for us himself.

During the last few days he spent in Havana he seemed somewhat tense. Once we came to his house and he wasn't there: his wife, Cucusa, very nervously told us that he was meeting with Fidel and that she was worried.

"Patricio is going to tell him things he doesn't want to hear about the war in Angola," she said.

When Patricio came back we asked him how it had gone. He told us: "He didn't respond at all. He was in a very bad mood."

It was not a subject to pursue.

During one conversation with Patricio, we decided it would be better for us if Ileana and I got married before leaving for Angola. According to Cuban law, it would be problematic for Ileana to be able to go with me if we were not married. Since she was Tony de la Guardia's daughter we could have cut through the red tape, but it was better to respect the rules.

And so, on February 12, 1989, we had a very simple ceremony at her grandparents' house, to which only the closest family were invited, along with my sister Laura, Conchita, and Chacho, a very dear friend from Argentina who had recently left El Salvador after fighting there for four years and who now agreed to be my best man. It was my first marriage, although I had five children. We all went afterward to Patricio's house to make merry. Drinking toast after toast, we ended up discussing the war in El Salvador—not a very appropriate subject for a wedding day. We had a picture taken of us together under an enormous portrait of Che in Patricio's living room.

A few days later, as we prepared to leave for Angola, I could tell Tony was uncomfortable about Ileana going with me.

"You go first to get things ready," he said in our telephone talks.

When I asked why this was necessary, he ventured something about Ileana's fragile health and the diseases in Africa. I decided to go to his house and talk to him man to man, and I caught him by surprise while he was painting. This was his passion. Despite his multiple occupations he always arranged, when he was in Havana, to paint every day between six and seven in the evening.

As young men, he and Patricio had studied art in the United States. All of Tony's friends had his pictures, and he had sold some of his etchings in Japan. He was initially inspired by Central American primitive art, but after his stay in Nicaragua his style evolved in the direction of folk art. During the 1980s there was briefly a free market in artwork and handicrafts in Havana's Cathedral Plaza. Tony was there selling his paintings every Saturday, wearing short pants and a T-shirt, set up with his table amidst the Bohemians. A colonel from the Ministry of the Interior! It was rumored that some of his superiors were uneasy— artists did not have a good reputation among the Cuban nomenklatura.

That was Tony: Saturdays with his paintings in the Cathedral Plaza, Sundays meticulously cleaning and polishing his weapons.

On this afternoon, I took him away from his paintbrushes and canvases, out into the garden where he felt comfortable dealing with important problems. I told him: "Look, chief, Ileana may be your daughter but she is also my wife. If all your officers travel with their wives, why can't I? She is coming with me."

He tried to argue with me. Then, seeing it was no use, he forced a weak smile and shrugged: "You're right. You can leave together the day after tomorrow. Take care of her."

THE FLIGHT TO LUANDA LEFT at six in the morning. When we got to the airport Tony was already waiting there to say goodbye to us, or, more correctly, to say goodbye to Ileana. Despite his efforts to pretend otherwise, his irritation with me over our garden conversation had not completely dissipated; his nervousness showed. As we proceeded up the Jetway to board the plane, we saw him running, very agitated, after us. He seized a bottle of vitamins from his uniform pocket and gave it to Ileana.

When we arrived in Luanda, Patricio's chauffeur was there waiting for us. He took us directly to Patricio, who greeted us warmly and got down to business, bringing us up to date about the game plan we were supposed to follow.

My primary job would involve consolidating relations with the director of the port of Luanda, whom we needed to work with in order to set up a maritime transport business along the African coast. I would be reincarnated as the representative of Merbar, Cuba's import-export business for such items as clothing, liquor and electronic goods.

Dining one night with Patricio, I remarked half-jokingly that our presence in Angola didn't seem much like that of an army of liberation; and I described the scene of press-gang recruitment by the Angolan army I had accidentally witnessed on my first visit. He acknowledged my point: while he thought it right that we had helped the Angolans wage an anticolonial struggle against the South Africans, it seemed disastrous that we should be involved in a civil war against UNITA; moreover, he admitted that the Cuban presence was about to become a scandal and that many Angolans wanted us to get out; it had been a mistake to confuse Angola with Nicaragua, for that matter, or any other country of Latin America, which of course had entirely different histories and social structures. We should definitely not be supporting an unpopular regime.

Prompted by Patricio's candor, I frankly confessed to him what I thought about Cuba's endemic problems. He freely acknowledged that without doubt there was far too much rigidity both in the management of the economy and in the political leadership of the people. He considered it imperative that there be an opening-up like the one that was occurring in the USSR and elsewhere in the socialist camp at that time.

I told him of my misgivings about our young people's lack of motivation. He responded with these exact words: "We ourselves are guilty. We have been incapable of offering them anything that will inspire them to take over for us."

My work as a commercial representative required me to go to the Republic of the Congo (Brazzaville), where we were planning to extend the activities of Merbar. Once upon a time, Che himself had journeyed up the river à la Conrad; I traveled far less romantically on a military cargo plane. I took advantage of the occasion to bring back a shipment of ivory that Colonel Laín, the man in charge of the Ministry of the Interior's Angola mission, had previously put down money for. (Ivory smuggling was an obvious way for Cuban officers to support the Revolution and themselves at the same time.) Patricio had also handed me a large quantity of West African francs so that I could change them into dollars for the account of Lieutenant Colonel Cuba, aide-de-camp to General Leopoldo Cintra Fría.

The trip lasted only two days. Back in Luanda, I dispatched the ivory by diplomatic pouch to the headquarters of the DGI (General Intelligence Agency), with instructions to forward it to Tony, who would be in charge of its resale in Mexico. From then on I was "our man" in charge of purchasing and transporting ivory: elephant tusks, but also carvings bought on the "white market"—so called after the color of ivory. No piece was sold at a fixed price; you had to haggle for each and every one of them.

When I entered the headquarters of the Ministry of the Interior in Brazzaville with my bundle of merchandise, I started to make a detailed list, item by item, stating the prices I had paid in West African francs. Colonel Laín watched me for a minute and then suggested that I inflate the prices somewhat. I told him that they had asked me to indicate the real prices, to which he responded that I should "live and let live."

He was the one who had actually been in charge of any negotiations until then, naturally purchasing everything with cash.

"That's not live and let live," I told him. "That's live and let rob!"

Back again in Luanda, I told Patricio about the incident. Scanning the list of prices I had paid for the ivories, he realized they were 50 percent lower than previous prices for equivalent merchandise. From this time on, I was invariably in charge of this particular racket, and made repeated trips to Congo, one of them with Ileana. There I stumbled upon a capitalist partner for Merbar, a storage place for the merchandise, and an outlet where we could actually sell the electronics we imported from Panama.

In May, I had just returned from another ivory trip when Patricio informed me that he had received a telegram ordering him to return permanently to Havana. This seemed very strange to us; during his last stay in Cuba they had informed him that he would be stationed in Angola until 1993. But it was a decision from the high command and he had no recourse but to follow orders.

Patricio had free airline tickets to Zimbabwe that the Cuban ambassador had sent him; he was too busy to make the trip and suggested that Ileana and I use them. We could see the country and hopefully bring back samples of valuable ivories ornamented with gold and silver that Havana had asked for.

We went to Harare. The DGI station chief and the ambassador were waiting for us at the airport. We stayed at the ambassador's residence, along with Alcibiades Hidalgo, the vice minister for foreign relations, who was then a member of the negotiating team at the Angola peace talks.

Next day I requested an audience with the ambassador. When I told him about my mission to bring back certain costly artifacts, he seemed astonished: he apparently thought I had come to Zimbabwe as a tourist. He told me that I could obtain all the information I wanted but could not take out any jewels—it was illegal! At this point, Alci-biades Hidalgo intervened to inform him that my missions were authorized by the Ministry of the Interior, that what I was asking for was part of my official duty, and that it might be better not to put impediments in my path. The ambassador quickly got a knowing look in his eyes.

We remained about one week in Zimbabwe. We made the pur-chases and transported them in our suitcases. Among other treasures, we carried some zebra skins, acquired at the request of General Colomé Ibarra to decorate his Havana apartment.

In Luanda once again, we were informed by comrades of MC that Tony had been replaced as our man in charge of commercial inter-ests. A telegram had just arrived from Havana asking us to return as quickly as possible. Patricio had already left.

I was pleased; these business functions had grown tiresome and I was eager to return to the world of intrigue that defined my life as a revolutionary.

I only had to resolve the logistics of the trip and the matter of money with General Rodilés of the Cuban army. There was no con-flict. He merely asked me, on behalf of General "Polo" Cintra Fría, to make one last trip to Congo before I left. He had located two elephant tusks that he wanted me to take back as a present to Raúl Castro, Fidel's brother and defense minister. The problem was that they had-n't yet been carved, and carvings from Congo were better than those from Angola. He wanted to have them crafted in the former and at the same time have me again change a quantity of West African francs into dollars. I insisted that this was not within my official role and that I had been urgently recalled to Havana.

We left for Cuba. Upon arrival, through one of the enterprises of Merbar, I sent the ivories to General Santiago, who had taken over for Tony at MC.

It was early June of 1989. Within days, Tony and Patricio would be under arrest.

14

HAVANA, JUNE–JULY 1989

HAVE ALREADY TOLD OF WATCHING Patricio's house being ransacked and of the state security man who asked me if I lacked faith in the Revolution. I was too stupefied by what I saw even to consider the question at that moment, though it would grow in my imagination in light of the even more grotesque events to come.

Ileana and I stood there gaping while the agents finished their violent shakedown of the house. Later we went to Tony's house, where the same scene had been played out and where also we were refused entry.

I accompanied Ileana and Patricio's son to the dread prison at Villa Marista, where we were met by someone named Major Blanco. He explained to us that Patricio and Tony were not prisoners but rather "detainees." We demanded to know where Tony was, but they told us they could not answer that question. Ileana wanted to know if she could contact a lawyer and when they would authorize visits. Major Blanco was unable to answer her questions, telling us that he did not know the reasons for the arrests. He simply repeated that we should not worry and that we should have full confidence in the Revolution.

Later on I understood what he was *really* saying: that we should have faith in Fidel. Fidel *was* the Revolution. He was its author, its judge and its reason for being. If Tony and Patricio were locked up it was because he had decided it was necessary. To question the Revolution was to question Fidel—and vice versa. That was the invariable answer to my questions. I could hardly complain: had I not myself often repeated that same stupid mantra?

We decided to go back to Tony's house, assuming that by then they would have finished their search. When we got there I suddenly realized that we ourselves were now objects of surveillance—to prevent us, I suppose, from alerting lawyers and the foreign press.

The next day, June 14, the official newspaper *Granma* published a press release from the Ministry of the Revolutionary Armed Forces. There was no mention of Tony or Patricio. But it announced the arrest of General Arnoldo Ochoa "for serious acts of corruption and the improper use of financial resources."

This was a bombshell. Ochoa was the most famous military figure in Cuba, a man of mythic stature.

Two days later, there was a long editorial in *Granma* under the headline "A True Revolution Never Permits Impunity." It announced that "several persons" had been arrested in connection with misdeeds blamed on Ochoa, including Diocles Torralvas, who was then minister of transportation. Patricio and Tony were finally named in this report. Drug trafficking was also mentioned for the first time: "Ochoa and some officials of the Ministry of the Interior who are connected to him made contact with international drug traffickers, made deals and intended to cooperate with, or may even have cooperated with, drug trafficking operations in Cuban territory."

Six days later, on June 22, *Granma* published a new editorial in an accusatory tone under the headline "We Know How to Cleanse Outrages Such As This in an Exemplary Manner." It was surely written by Fidel himself. It reported that when Ochoa and the de la Guardia brothers were arrested ten days earlier, "there was no information about activities related to drug trafficking. The investigations were aimed at facts having to do with illicit business, corruption, immorality and other errors and irregularities by Ochoa, in which Patricio and Tony de la Guardia appeared to be closely connected." The anonymous author of the editorial specified that for some time there had been "rumors" among friends of Cuba and increasingly threatening accusations about drugs coming from the United States government. An investigation had been "under way" and it was no surprise that action had to be taken.

What surprised me about this affair had nothing to do with the "revelations" related to drug trafficking, but rather the sudden use of these accusations against the arrested men. Indeed, the issue of drug trafficking was nothing new. On the contrary, it was a matter that was much commented on, if not among the people, at least within the various sectors of the state apparatus, and when it was spoken of, no one was scandalized. It was, after all, one more way of "making war on imperialism."

The rumors about Cuban drug traffic had peaked years earlier, toward the end of the 1970s. The U.S. Drug Enforcement Agency had denounced Cuba for these activities on several occasions. But it was not until 1982 that a United States Senate committee declared that "for the first time there is detailed and reliable information connecting Cuba to trafficking in drugs and arms." Because of that investigation, a vice admiral and member of the Central Committee of the Communist Party, Aldo Santamaría was indicted by the North Americans for drug trafficking. So were others: Fernando Ravelo and Gonzalo Bassols, who were respectively ambassador and first counselor at the Cuban embassy in Colombia; and René Rodríguez, also a member of the Central Committee and the president of the Cuban Institute for Friendship Among Peoples.

At this time everyone knew that Robert Vesco, a crook and drug merchant and a friend of Fidel Castro's, was living in Havana. Under indictment for securities fraud in the United States, he had been given "humanitarian asylum" in Cuba and had been authorized to build a luxury house, with a private pier for his yacht, on an island off the coast called Cayo Largo del Sur. It was widely rumored that money laundering and drug operations had been planned there.

Cuba had also given protection to Jaime Guillot Lara, another notorious trafficker, who was arrested in Mexico and who in spite of being under indictment in Colombia and in the United States, was finally turned over by the Mexican Foreign Ministry because of pressure from the Cuban government. Guillot Lara later appeared in Havana, moving into the same neighborhood as Vesco.

And before that, drug trafficking by Fernando Ravelo, who served not only in Colombia but also in Nicaragua, was such a public matter that he was expelled from the latter country following the publication of a photograph in which he could be seen prominently placed among the invitees to the baptism of Guillot Lara's son in Bogotá. In the same manner, high-level contacts were authorized by Havana with one of the biggest Colombian dealers, Carlos Lehder, to obtain his financing for the purchase of two aircraft specially equipped for presidential travel. The original drug impresario of the 1970s, Lehder handed over one of the planes, which remained parked, visible to the entire world, for more than a year at the José Martí International Airport in Havana.

This was the context in which the arrests and sudden indignation about drugs had to be seen. For more than thirty years, Cuba had been under threat and subject to a trade embargo. The MC service had received orders to break the embargo and to obtain hard currency. Who in his right mind could not have foreseen that such an order must inevitably lead to collaboration with all kinds of smugglers and criminals from both Americas who have operated for centuries in the waters of the Caribbean? And that such a pirate mentality among lawless Panamanians, Colombians and privateers from the United States must inevitably intersect with drug traffic? The Cubans who found themselves implicated in drugs were following the very logic of the two most important missions they had been given by the government: to break the embargo and bring in cash.

At the beginning of 1989, rumors emanating from the United States implicating Cuba in drug trafficking became more and more persistent. *Newsweek* published an article that laid out the case for Cuban involvement. For the first Bush administration this became a powerful argument against the Castro government. No wonder the highest levels of government in Havana, worried about a possible U.S. response, were looking for prominent figures to scapegoat.

All this notwithstanding, the accusations in *Granma* were incoherent. When Ochoa, Tony, Patricio and the others were arrested on June 12, nothing was mentioned about drug trafficking; at this time their sin was still "corruption." The drug issue was not to be "discovered" until after the first interrogations. Yet we were all wondering, What was the reason for the simultaneous arrests and for the strange charges brought against the accused men? The *Granma* editorial of June 22 provided the depressing answer: the accused had not only endangered Cuba's prestige but also threatened "the security of our country." That crime carried the death penalty. To add more weight to the official nature of the accusation, the editorial noted that it was not expressing its opinion alone, but also that of the Central Committee of the Communist Party, the commander in chief, the Revolutionary Armed Forces and the Ministry of the Interior.

It was a revolutionary version of Alice in Wonderland: first the verdict, then the trial.

I SPOKE WITH MY FRIENDS, with officials of the Ministry of the Interior, and with Tony's colleagues. Most of them did not believe a word of the charges. Others fled as if they were running away from the plague. "Bolshevik," my old instructor in my first military course, visited us in a show of solidarity. Gestures such as his comforted us immensely.

I felt incapable of reflecting. I experienced the same sensation of standing outside myself that I had felt when I was carrying out an armed operation and seemed to be watching myself as if in a film. At the same time, I did my best to calculate and coolly plan out a defense. I sought a meeting with the minister of the interior, José Abrantes, and with General Colomé Ibarra, then chief of military counterintelligence, who had been on the doomed operation when my father was killed. Both refused. Only Piñeiro agreed to receive me—at three o'clock in the morning. He repeated the official story. I called him a cynic.

"Don't you see?" he said. "They are involved in trafficking operations that involve countries with which we have official relations."

Such hypocrisy made me indignant. Hadn't he spent his entire life mounting illegal operations in countries with which we had official relations?

"Don't worry about yourself," he told me. "I've verified that you have nothing to do with this story."

"Thanks," I replied.

After about two weeks, Tony and Patricio were finally authorized to receive visits from their wives and children. Both of them asked their families not to hire lawyers. This was a problem purely among *compañeros* and it would be resolved among *compañeros*.

I was not related by blood to the de la Guardia brothers and did not participate in the visits. When Ileana returned, she told me that her father had seemed very tense, and at the same time in a kind of unconscious state. When she asked him if he knew anything about an upcoming trial, he looked at her blankly and said no.

That very night Ileana received a telephone call from the Ministry of the Interior asking her to come to the central office of the Ministry of the Revolutionary Armed Forces the next day at nine in the morning, where a public trial would take place. Only the immediate family was authorized to attend. A little later they called again to indicate that the trial would not begin until two in the afternoon. I was not allowed in the courtroom, but I accompanied the de la Guardias to it. A car followed us without letting us out of its sight for an instant. I called counterintelligence and asked why they were tailing us. They told me that it was to ensure the protection of family members.

WHAT CAN I SAY ABOUT THE TRIAL, that month of dementia and nightmares?

Every day, the videotaped courtroom session of the day before was nationally televised. Ileana and I were staying with her grandparents; we prevented them from watching the legalized murder that was being

cooked up. The assault on the defendants was total, including issu-
ing the twins exactly the same clothing to link them in crime and
deny their individual identities. Watching television, I tried to look
past the images in case a fragment of the truth accidentally slipped
through the stage-managed proceedings.

The cross-examination was nauseating. Military heroes were on
trial, after all, and to win over the public, the prosecution presented
the issue as one involving the abuse of privilege by an elite. (Never
mind that the judges themselves enjoyed the same privileges, or even
greater ones, than the defendants.) It was as if the system sat in judg-
ment of itself, seeking to repair its corruption in an act of hypocriti-
cal exorcism. To really put privilege on trial in Cuba one would have
had to start at the very top and work systematically down.

Like so many other communist show trials in recent memory, this
one kept its secrets coded within a deadly language game of newspeak
and doubletalk.

With a sort of Freudian slip meant to reassure the public that the
defendants were not being coerced, an editorial in *Granma* stated:
"Our Revolution has never used violent methods to obtain information and it will never use them; this is an inviolable rule." Nevertheless, the defendants were in fact submitted to systematic torture. Not
to obtain the truth, of course, but rather to guarantee that they would
lie.

In a letter that Patricio managed to smuggle out of prison a couple of years later, he told the story:

> During the thirty-three days that the entire trial lasted, including
> the subsequent days until we signed the final documents recording
> our penalties—in other words, from June 12 until July 15—I was
> not permitted to sleep because every twenty or thirty minutes they
> awakened me by opening and slamming shut the door to my cell.
> The exact time I remained awake I cannot exactly say because of
> my exhausted mental state, but it was more or less that period. And
> they had taken away my watch. What I am certain of is that I
> remained awake all night because of the opening and closing of the
> door. . . . These were not my imaginings because I knew already that
> this method of psychological pressure was in use at Villa Marista
> since the previous year, when Kundi Pahama [Angola's Minister of
> State Security] visited Cuba and made a working visit to Villa Marista.
> Everything was explained to us because I was Pahama's advisor in
> Angola and accompanied him on that visit when Colonel Blanco
> Oropesa gave us a tour with an explanation of the methods they
> used.

While I was in prison I was not permitted to consult with any lawyer in the five days after I was arrested, which the law requires. In short, during the twenty-odd days that the trial and the interrogations lasted I remained in a state of shock. At no time was I given a medical examination. I became an idiot who believed everything that he was told and that he was accused of doing. I admitted crimes that I did not commit, such as having given away I don't know how many cars that were later confiscated and had to be returned. I accused myself of crimes that I did not commit and of which there was never any proof to convict me except for my own words. . . . During that entire period in which I remained in confinement without any advice from a defense lawyer, I felt stupefied, with my mind frozen like a zombie's. I had to read documents three or four times to understand what they said. I fell into a profound state of depression.

One day they took me out in the morning and ordered me to convince my family not to seek out a lawyer or go to the Human Rights Commission, that this would hurt us and that the Revolution would defend us as the revolutionaries that we were, that the Revolution would not apply the law of Saturn, etc. etc. I was taken to a house in Siboney and there I spoke for the first time with my family and convinced them that they should not worry and should not go to any lawyer nor to the Human Rights Commission. What an imbecile I was! How I let myself be deceived! I was still a romantic and a dreamer.

International human rights organizations have documented the fact that sleep deprivation is one of the cruelest forms of torture, producing an incapacity to think and act in a rational way. If it is enough to deprive someone of sleep for twenty-four to seventy-two hours in order to produce such a result, the same treatment applied over thirty-three days would have made Tony and Patricio ready to admit anything.

According to Article 26 of the Cuban Law of Military Justice, every defendant "may designate to represent and defend him a lawyer, a military officer, a representative of a social organization to which he belongs, or he may assume his own defense." Nevertheless, the indictment against the brothers said: "Despite the fact that none of the defendants designated a civilian lawyer for his defense, they were assigned military lawyers as their defenders." In other words, the defendants in the Ochoa/de la Guardia trials effectively had no defense worthy of that name.

The transcript is filled with testimony that casts doubt on the legitimacy of the procedure. Among this testimony is that of Patricio, who, pressured by the chief judge to express his concerns, makes a statement that sounds like something out of Koestler's masterpiece, *Darkness at Noon:*

> During these days I have read some reports in the foreign press, in which certain gentlemen from a commission of human rights have mentioned my name and that of my brother, and that of some *compañeros,* with great concern for our situation. According to the report I have read, they claim that we have been tortured physically and mentally; they claim that we have been kept incommunicado, that we have been exposed to great pressure, that our family has been exposed to police pressure and I don't know how many other lies and outrages. I want to say to the *compañeros* who are present here, that since the first moment in which they arrested me, they treated me as I didn't deserve to be treated: They treated me with the greatest respect, the greatest consideration and the greatest attention. At no time have we been incommunicado. Each time that I have wanted something, I asked for it and they brought it to me. I asked for my defense attorney. I have known this major for many years. And at no time has anyone pressured me to do anything, nor to say what I said, nor to confess to anything that I did. I have confessed because I wanted to.

Patricio's smuggled letter, dated October 5, 1991, sounds very different:

> After twenty-three days, I was taken from the cell at midday and they took me to one of the interrogation rooms which has a hidden listening device where a major from the Ministry of the Interior was waiting. I thought that he was another interrogator, but he turned out to be the lawyer assigned by the Ministry to defend me. I recognized his face but, in reality, I had never spoken with him before. He introduced himself by telling me who he was, what his job was and that for him it was a disgrace to have to defend me but he would try to do it to the best of his ability. With this happy introduction, I asked him when the trial was and he told me it was that very afternoon, within two or three hours, and that he did not have much time to get ready with me. Right there I responded that if that was the case, he was wasting his time with me, because that way I had no defense at all, I was indefensible. I realized that everything was already prepared beforehand.... The lawyer asked me what my awards and decorations had been and what internationalist missions or special training I had completed, giving me to

understand that he had not even had access or time to study my
résumé of thirty years of struggle and even less time to read the
indictment itself.... The time we spent in our meeting was no more
than twenty or thirty minutes.

Thus as you can see I was not even permitted the legal defense
that everyone is entitled to by law, as our socialist constitution pro-
claims. They deceived my elderly parents, my children and my wife,
by telling them that we would have a good defense lawyer. They
deceived us and they deceived the people.

In the transcript of the trial, the defense offered by this lawyer,
Major Julio Gonzáles Guethon, is contained in a single brief para-
graph: "As the defense attorney for Patricio de la Guardia Font, I declare
that my client did not participate in drug trafficking activities although
he did know about drug trafficking by his brother. We believe that
the punishment sought by the prosecution is extremely severe." And
he added that his client had committed an ethical lapse as a Communist and as an officer of the Ministry of the Interior, but that his
brother was the true wrongdoer. The lawyer referred to the career of
Patricio, to the cooperation he had rendered and to his sincere
repentance.

The accusations of the general prosecutor were a sinister farce. The
alleged crime was not so much having put the nation in danger as it
was having betrayed the trust of Fidel. A mortal sin, to be sure. Ochoa
was, in particular, unpardonable:

> As a trusted man, close to Fidel and to Raúl, he is an exceptional
> witness to all of their thoughts and he knew perfectly well the
> absolute correspondence between those thoughts and the official
> positions private and public of the Revolution. Above all Ochoa
> betrayed Fidel, about whom it is not sufficient to point out as a solid
> argument that he was his commander in chief.... Fidel is our voice,
> our representation, the one we return to in difficult moments.
>
> Mr. President, it is our professional duty to recognize that in the
> case of each of the accused there are mitigating circumstances, espe-
> cially the good conduct that they displayed prior to these events
> ... but at the same time, and with overwhelming evidence, there
> are concurrent aggravating circumstances from the moral and polit-
> ical point of view: their very attributes and their high positions are
> what makes the cases against Ochoa and the de la Guardia broth-
> ers even stronger.

Everything had already been said in the editorial in *Granma* immediately following the arrest. After that the newspaper continued to

set the tone, saying that the offenses of the defendants did not merely involve political activities. Their treason was of another kind and very grave: "... against the morals, the principles, the laws, and the prestige of our Revolution, of our glorious and heroic Revolutionary Armed Forces and the Ministry of the Interior. This type of treason always leads sooner or later to political treason."

It was revolutionary logic: even if those under arrest had not committed treason, they were destined to do it. Their treason was under way within their minds. They were already "objectively" guilty.

WAS THERE ANYTHING OF SUBSTANCE in this accusation?

General Arnoldo Ochoa, the central figure in the trial, was accused of having dedicated himself to personal business activities instead of worrying about his military mission in Angola, of having $200,000 in a bank account in Panama, and of having prepared important drug trafficking operations upon his return from Angola. As for Tony, they accused him of having organized, in 1987, seventeen drug trafficking operations by the Colombians aimed at the United States—operations that had produced a profit of six million dollars in cash, a sum whose ultimate destination was never brought up. Where were these millions? No one ever accused Tony of having taken this money; the prosecutor never claimed it was in some numbered bank account.

The indictment and interrogation were aimed at discrediting Ochoa and minimizing the importance of his previous service on behalf of the Revolution. In Fidel's description, Ochoa was an idiot without political ideas, motivated only by a desire for profit and personal enrichment. Fidel similarly tried to minimize the revolutionary work done by the de la Guardia brothers, even to the point of denying that Tony had participated in the war in Nicaragua.

What cynicism! I saw Tony with my own eyes on the southern front in Nicaragua. And I know he entered Somoza's bunker.

It wasn't enough for them to take his life, they also had to take his past and his reputation, and what he had done in the Nicaraguan guerrilla war, among the proudest achievements of his life.

Fidel also explained to writer Gianni Minna that the codefendant José Abrantes had been named minister of the interior simply because of seniority, not because he had particular talent. Fidel neglected to say that before being minister, Abrantes was the original chief of Fidel's personal security force, so dedicated to this task that he slept on a mattress in front of the door of whatever room the commander in chief slept in. During those years, Fidel had time enough to get to know him intimately. And who, in any case, could ever believe that in Cuba someone can be named minister of the interior against Fidel Castro's wishes?

What had happened in Ochoa's expedition in Angola was clear, despite the fog this trial set out to create. Cuba embarked on that adventure during the Brezhnev era, when Soviet imperialism was at its height following the United States defeat in Vietnam. In the agreed-upon division of roles, Cuba was to supply the troops and the Soviets the supplies. The war was prolonged and Brezhnev left the scene. His successor Andropov disappeared as well, and fifty thousand Cuban soldiers remained in Angola under precarious conditions. Ochoa found himself in the position of a latter-day Roman proconsul, obliged to feed his troops and execute his battle plans, knowing perfectly well that he could not count on financial support from the Soviets or anyone else. In the trial he was reproached for having bought and sold on the black market, but how could he have done otherwise? Food products came from Cuba in cans; he had to trade these rations for fresh vegetables and meat on the black market. Everyone did it and all the officers and responsible officials knew about it. The elephant ivory tusks that were bought in the Congo Republic were sent back to Cuba on military planes to be sold later in Mexico by MC. The Ministry of the Interior and the Ministry of the Revolutionary Armed Forces divided up the proceeds of these deals openly, in front of everyone. I myself was once assigned to leave Angola in a military aircraft with large bags of tusks on either side, without even being asked to keep this cargo a secret.

And what about that $200,000 account Ochoa had in Panama? Half belonged to the Sandinistas for an arms sale. They themselves confirmed it by letter during the trial, without omitting an expression of their open hostility toward the prosecution. Ochoa might have had thousands of dollars in one account, in the same way that Tony had thousands in cash. These sums may seem substantial, but they are minor in relation to the extent of the operations they were "running" at any given moment. In secret operations it is necessary to have cash on hand to be able to act swiftly; it is the way the Cuban system works—with people in charge of important operations funding them out of their own proprietary accounts. For Fidel to use against Ochoa and Patricio and Tony a system he himself had put in place was a savage irony indeed.

THE LAST TIME THAT I SAW GENERAL OCHOA was at Patricio's house. At that time there was already a sense that something was happening, something invisible but menacing—an unfavorable atmosphere developing around this soldier. That night in particular, I remember that Ochoa spent a long time speaking about perestroika: about the need to discuss our problems openly, to be able to travel and talk freely. I remember that Patricio also mentioned perestroika with admiration. And more than once I surprised him while he was reading Gorbachev's book. An interest in perestroika, rather than an excess of cash on hand, was a key element in this trial.

The other, of course, was the question of drugs.

They accused Tony of having organized seventeen different operations related to drugs on Cuban territory, and they accused Ochoa of having overseen contact with the notorious Colombian drug lord Pablo Escobar. These accusations were made as if there were no context into which they fit. But the fact is that many people knew about the presence of high-speed boat operators—smugglers—in Cuba. Many suspected that the secret comings and goings of these modern privateers were not part of legal import-export businesses or, at the very least, that these businesses employed highly unorthodox methods.

The supposed drug schemes of Ochoa were fictitious. A document presented during the trial enumerates seventeen operations and gives the dates, volume, participants and sums involved with exhaustive precision—an excess of detail calculated to make Tony's confessions sound evasive by comparison. But in trying too hard to prove the case, the state managed to arouse doubts.

A few of these alleged operations:

- April 1987: 400 kilos of cocaine for $325,000. The landing of an airplane in Varadero, the handover in a house in Villa Tortuga and the delivery of a boat.
- At the end of the same month, 500 kilos of cocaine at a price of $250,000, thrown from an airplane fourteen miles from the Cruz del Padre lighthouse.
- March 1989: 400 kilos of cocaine priced at $500,000, thrown from an airplane twenty miles from the Bay of Cádiz.
- April 1989: Cocaine priced at $250,000 detected in territorial waters next to Cuba when a boat broke up on the north coast. It was repaired in Barlovento and went from there to Varadero. It was offloaded to another boat on the small island and returned to Varadero.

There are problems with this documentation. The zone around Villa Tortuga, in Varadero, near one of Fidel's personal residences, is under military control; and Barlovento, off limits to foreigners, is also subject to intense surveillance. In general, it is hard to imagine that this stream of boats and planes could have lasted for three years without full knowledge of the armed forces and the highest state authorities.

It may come as a surprise that seasoned militants, among them high-level cadres, could have participated for several years in these operations without asking awkward questions. But such things happen in a kingdom of doubletalk. In Cuba, for example, the official discourse never ceases to denounce inequality, yet everyone knows that this doesn't prevent the existence of privileges. Similarly, the official party line has no words harsh enough to condemn drug trafficking, but when men like Robert Vesco, Jaime Guillot Lara and Carlos Lehder support the Revolution they become not only useful allies but socially acceptable friends.

This doubletalk is part of the system. Everything that one can do in favor of the Revolution is legitimate and moral. When Fidel embraces the Spanish minister of the interior who executed the revolutionary Julión Grimau, there's no problem. When he presents medals to members of that same Bolivian military junta that executed Che Guevara, there's no problem.

IT IS SAD TO READ ARNALDO OCHOA'S deposition when he appears before the Military Tribunal and declares that the report of the prosecutor is much more complete than any he himself could have made:

> The first thing that I must say is that, in my judgment, there came a time when I turned away from the right road of the Revolution's objectives, but I think that was the way it was. I have analyzed this a great deal, although I can tell you that I have not formed conclusions about everything; but I have thought there are so many irresponsible actions, and if you wish, actions of corruption. Because what right did I have to handle any kind of money? Something that I never had done in my life; I was never an ambitious man, nor have I gone around with a lot of money, I didn't lack for anything at all. And I could tell you as well that there came a time in my military life when I also felt tired. That is to say, I am not, objectively, the same man who the prosecutor was saying fought here and led there. I even felt burned out. Many times in Angola itself I found myself in very difficult situations, very difficult, very complicated

for me. I think that along with so many years, how should we say, of acting alone, I took the wrong road, I lost a little bit of contact with reality. Because also it has been said on many occasions that I was not working. That is not the case. I made a great effort to accomplish things; I couldn't fulfill all my duties; many think that I devoted myself only to business. That was not true either....

The tone, downcast and humbled, is different from that of Ochoa's previous testimony before the Tribunal of Honor, where he emphasized prouder emotions of remorse and sacrifice.* By the time of his appearance before the Military Tribunal he is already a condemned man who meditates aloud in an attempt to understand what has happened to him. There is, however, a certain continuity between the two appearances. In the first one, Ochoa said: "One begins with something and begins with details in one's life, and I would say that beginning by grumbling when they give you an order ends with the thought that everything that comes from the high command is wrongly ordered. And on that road one begins to think independently and to believe that you yourself are the one who is right."

Until Angola, Ochoa had never had to shoulder alone the weighty problems of feeding his troops and assuring their deployment, without material support from Havana. Now he had to take care of business with whatever means came to hand, and as long as problems didn't surface, the chain of command would turn a blind eye.

After the victory over South African troops at Cuito Cuanavale, regarded as the greatest feat of arms in Cuban history after the Bay of Pigs, Arnoldo Ochoa was in the typical situation of a military governor. More than three hundred thousand Cubans had passed through Angola, many of them spending several years there. Little by little they were discovering that the war of liberation was not as they had imagined. Angola was not Cuba, nor even Nicaragua. The war was not leading to socialism in Africa; indeed, many of the indigenous combatants were not volunteers but forcibly recruited slaves. And the Cubans were not much appreciated by those they were allegedly helping: for the Angolan people, the Cuban presence meant the continuation of war, when their deepest desire was for peace.

---

*The Tribunal of Honor stripped the defendants of their ranks and expelled them from the army. The Military Tribunal tried them on the charges brought against them.

In these conditions, despite military victories, the return home felt nothing like a triumph, and the combatants did not feel like heroes. The Cuban soldiers returned from battles whose meaning they did not understand, to be sent to new "fronts": in construction or the harvest or some other demeaning activity. And after they had left, the counterrevolutionary enemy of yesterday, led by Jonas Savimbi, moved into Luanda and commandeered the abandoned residence of their general, Arnoldo Ochoa.

Despite this defeat, Ochoa returned from Angola with immense prestige and popularity among the troops, which explains why the judges and Fidel himself went to such extravagant lengths to diminish the importance of his past works and achievements. The prosecutor said in his closing argument: "Some literary figures, judges, and I myself, have been wondering what happened to the other Ochoa, that is, the hero, the competent military chief, the young *compañero* who took part in the invasion with Camilo Cienfuegos in January of 1959. We were going in senseless circles until this trial revealed that the old Ochoa no longer exists, that the old Ochoa has dissolved into the grotesque caricature that we have had before us during these last days."

Fidel Castro stepped up the revisionism in his interview with Gianni Minna: "No. Ochoa absolutely did not participate during the insurrectional struggle of the Sandinistas. . . . He was sent much later to Nicaragua to advise on the organization of the Sandinista Army." And with respect to the leadership of operations in Angola: "The fundamental decisions were taken in Cuba. . . . We had *compañeros* who had to carry out the orders, instructions and plans of the high command over there. . . . The leadership of the military operations was here in Cuba. . . . Ochoa at that time was very inefficient. . . . We gave him a general administrative mission but not the direction of troops. . . ."

Which demands the question: if Ochoa's assigned role was more administrative than operational, why was he accused precisely of having neglected operational tasks in favor of administrative matters? No less paradoxical are Fidel's own clumsy ruminations concerning the merits of collective leadership and his self-conscious posturing with regard to the dangers of a personalized leadership style:

> All the missions in Angola, in Ethiopia and wherever, were the responsibility in the first instance of the Party leadership and of the high command of our Revolutionary Armed Forces. If anything went wrong, it was our responsibility, absolutely ours, and we are not going to blame any particular officer, any particular military leader. That was the way and it cannot be any other way. There is a tendency in the

world to individualize success. The very successes of the Revolution are often attributed to me. [But] the successes of Castro are the successes of the entire people and the successes of the entire leadership.

In Africa, Ochoa had to resist pressures and orders from a general staff that was leaning over maps thousands of miles away while he daily had to face enormous practical difficulties. He justified the need for foreign currency by constructing two military airports. Let's remember also that he was, of course, habituated to tacit understandings with Havana and to free expenditure of money without having to leave written records.

None of the alleged self-enrichment was reflected in his lifestyle, and on this count the tribunal's accusations are extremely vague. It is true that in foreign involvements such as the war in Angola one sees much cash circulating, including large amounts of foreign currency. It goes without saying that the borderline between the moral and the immoral may sometimes seem hazy. Corruption does not begin with the decision to embezzle funds; it gradually gains ground and takes over in an insidious way as one accrues certain small favors and privileges. It might begin by accompanying a smuggler from abroad who offers you a certain service in a special store: you return to the store with your family. You get used to travel, restaurants, conditions of life that are not those of the average Cuban and, to justify them, you look for any explanation that comes to hand.

Fidel does not explain it any differently in his interview with Gianni Minna: "How does the process of corruption begin in these people? They travel, they go, they come, they buy, they bring, they carry away; and it's not that they do actual embezzlement; it's not that they have secreted away large amounts; rather they begin to be liberal in the purchasing of things, in the giving out of gifts, in their style of life, in their spending—in all of these things."

Is it accurate to conclude that such weaknesses opened the way to actual embezzlement of funds? The amounts in cash that were found in the homes of Tony's friends or in Ochoa's accounts in Panama do not confirm this. No one denied during the trial that the more than six million dollars collected from seventeen drug trafficking operations had been turned over to superior officers. But apparently it was not useful for testimony from recipient higher-ups to be publicly aired; hence, the trial featured no discussion of what the accused allegedly earned from their crimes.

PRIVILEGES? OF COURSE THERE ARE PRIVILEGES!

First, privileges in office. In a poor country subjected to rationing, the higher cadres of the regime have access to houses, vehicles, appliances and other conveniences without actually having to pay for them. These are goods that no one else can dream of acquiring, not even through the hardest labor. It was an open secret, now officially made public, that Carlos Aldana, a high official who voted for capital punishment for the defendants in the Ochoa/de la Guardia trial, had been receiving commissions from the Japanese firm Sony for more than eight years. And in his interview with Gianni Minna, Fidel brought up the case of a special clinic at the Ministry of the Interior in Pinar del Rio; as far as I know, that clinic was dedicated by Fidel himself and has never been merged into the general public health service. These special clinics are a common feature of life in Cuba. The most luxurious is Clinic 43, devoted to the members of the politburo, where even the aspirin is imported and where the patients enjoy a special menu.

Access to foreign exchange is another form of privilege. During missions abroad, high Cuban officials handle large amounts as they pass through international airports on their way to various parts of the world. Almost always there is only a vague boundary between public funds and private spending. The privileges that come from handling American dollars can be an insidious form of corruption. But it is another thing actually to embezzle funds or falsify accounts, something I witnessed in Congo.

The charges lodged against the accused, beginning with Ochoa, entailed having entered into a process of Mafia-like criminality. But in all the questioning of the accused, no facts were put forward upon which to base such an accusation.

Many factors came together in this trial. At that time the convulsions of perestroika and the upheaval in the socialist camp were on everyone's mind. From one fallback position to another, Cuba had been moving for years in a zigzag pattern in its political economy. Cuban troops had returned from Angola disillusioned about what they had been told would be a great internationalist odyssey. No one believed anymore in the miracles promised by the Maximum Leader and people were beginning to whisper jokes about the aging caudillo. What better way to deflect attention than suddenly to uncover a conspiracy among the most trusted military leaders in the country?

There was no plot to overthrow the government. It was rather that many years of semiclandestine struggle and shared danger had established ties of solidarity and trust outside official channels. I saw this firsthand many times. I was once invited to dine at the home of the minister of transportation, Diocles Torralvas, where Ochoa, Tony and Patricio were all together and I heard them speak of Fidel as though he were a crazy old man. Without a doubt the house was full of hidden listening devices. And they must have known this. But while they talked irreverently about El Jefe in the manner of men of action, they did not talk of plots.

The trial was essentially about the fact that in Cuba there is room for only one hero. Fidel understood far better than Ochoa himself how popular the general was in the army as a result of his career as a victorious military officer, and how his followers might react if an open political crisis were ever to break out. Upon his return from Angola, Ochoa was given command of Cuba's western military region. He had asked for the unified command of all three regions that, given his military achievements, was his due. But this would mean a conflict with Raúl Castro. It was a minefield that must have deeply worried Fidel, who, as always, took the initiative when confronted with a problem. Thus the editorial in *Granma,* so clearly bearing his fingerprints, put emphasis on the political treason that was said to flow from a breach of revolutionary principles. He was far ahead of the accused, who did not realize the symbolism they embodied as a potential force for change in Cuba, a symbolism Fidel understood entirely.

FIDEL CALLED OCHOA, TONY, PATRICIO and the rest of the accused "vulgar adventurers," despite the thirty years they had dedicated to his cause by executing special illegal missions he himself had ordered. The docile behavior of the defendants in front of the tribunal can be explained by the sleep deprivation and other torments visited on them during their detention. Yet I remain convinced that their stoic attitude also signified each was consciously rendering one last service to the Revolution. Their confessions and their self-criticisms showed how deep was that sense of duty internalized over so many years.

Here is Arnoldo Ochoa, Cuba's greatest soldier, speaking before the Military Honor Tribunal:

> I want to tell the *compañeros* that I believe I've betrayed the nation and I say it with all honesty, treason costs you your life.... Now, the man who is speaking to you here, because of everything that has happened, doesn't have the slightest doubt that he is a much cleaner revolutionary then the one of twenty days ago. Doesn't have

the slightest doubt. Modestly, whatever decision you may take in my case, you can rest assured that I will still be a revolutionary.... I believe that today the tribunal of my own conscience is the harshest judge of all.

Here is Tony de la Guardia, interrogated by the prosecutor at the Tribunal of Justice:

Q: How many officers knew about this business in Cuba?

A: The officials who are arrested here.

Q: Those and no other?

A: No one else as far as I know. As far as I know not one more.

Q: How far were you going to go with the drug trafficking?

A: Actually I was not going to take it very far. My interest was not in doing big drug operations, nor in making laboratories or anything. It was to be able to make a profit in hard currency.... I don't want to justify the damage I've done but ... in fact this year I was thinking about ceasing the drug operations, because the enterprises had already been created and taken on their own life, they had a base of capital that could produce hard currency and I didn't want to continue in drugs. I did not like that business.

Q: You have children, right?

A: Four children.

Q: Did you think of them during any of these operations when you were receiving dollars from drug trafficking and when you were stocking your business with drug traffickers? Did you think about the consequences of drug trafficking for the youth of the world?

A: In truth, I did not think about that.

Q: But you've traveled a great deal through the world.

A: Yes, sir.

Q: You've seen the misery.

A: Yes, sir.

Q: You have seen the consequences of drug trafficking.

A: Yes, sir.

Q: You've seen what it means for youth.

A: Correct.

Q: You know that it is a plague on humanity at this time.

A: Yes, sir.

Q: And you are part of that factory that causes misfortune in the world.

A: Yes, sir.

Q: And your conscience, de la Guardia?

A: It's very bad.

The first law of the revolutionary's life is the law of silence. Fidel personally visited Tony in his cell for three hours and asked him not to name any of his superiors during the trial. Everything had to stay in "the family."

One of the most notorious aspects of the trial is that at no time was there any mention of Interior Minister José Abrantes, the official tasked with overseeing all the activities of MC and of Tony de la Guardia. Fidel, his brother Raúl and Abrantes were not in the courtroom but followed the trial through a two-way mirror. Is it not curious that no one during the trial proposed the most natural thing in the world—that Abrantes be summoned to testify about Tony, who was his immediate subordinate?

Everything was done for Pepe Abrantes. The trial covered for him because in that way Fidel was covered. Nevertheless, his turn would come soon enough. There came a time when Abrantes would comment cryptically that he had always kept Fidel informed of *everything*. This elicited an infuriated response from the Castro brothers and caused Abrantes' abrupt fall from power; but this was too late to help the defendants.

WE FELT WE WERE LIVING within a nightmare. The days went by and justice proved expeditious: the tragedy accelerated toward its denouement. The trial before the Tribunal of Honor began on June 30. Starting July 3, *Granma* published a report every day. On July 4 began the trial proper in front of the Special Military Tribunal; on July 5 came the closing statement by the prosecutor; on July 7, the verdict of the Special Military Tribunal; on July 8, the Supreme Tribunal sentenced Arnoldo Ochoa, Antonio de la Guardia, Amado Padron Trujillo and Jorge Martínez Valdez to death. And on July 9 came confirmation of the sentences by the Council of State, headed, of course, by Fidel Castro himself.

Patricio alone escaped death: "Because in fact he had not committed nor was he connected to a single one of the crimes involving the most serious of the offenses which has been charged here, which is drug trafficking, constituting an act of treason." Nevertheless, Prosecutor Juan Escalona demanded a thirty-year sentence for him: "Perhaps Patricio, as an aggravating aspect of his responsibility, in fact knew of the conduct of his brother, the deeds that Tony de la Guardia had committed, drug trafficking in our country, and he lacked the moral courage and the integrity of a revolutionary general to denounce him in time."

Thirty years for not turning in his brother, who committed no crime!

Eighteen months later, Patricio, still trying to understand the consequences of the confessions he and the others had been coerced into making, and demanding a new trial, wrote from prison:

> Many people wonder why I lied and did not tell the truth at the trial. First, because when the day of the trial arrived they had turned me into an idiot who believed himself to be the worst criminal in the world. Second, because I wanted to save my brother Tony — because I had been warned that our punishment would depend on our cooperation in the trial and our acceptance of the charges against us — and since I was the last one to testify, I took into account the way in which the others had testified. I did not want to contradict them so as not to make things worse, because they would be the ones most affected. Third, because I wasn't a lawyer and because unfortunately I don't know anything about legal matters and trials and never had even the slightest advice from a defense attorney, I fell into the trap that we all fell into. . . . It may also be the case that I let myself be played for a fool because of what might happen to my twin brother. Who knows? I hope that someday some psychiatrist or psychologist can explain to me my stupid behavior in confessing to so many of the accusations and charges that were made against me. It's now too late to lament it, but not too late to reclaim my rights as a citizen and ask for a new trial, after two and a half years of prison.

It took me a while, but eventually I clearly saw what had delivered Tony to the firing squad: his friendship with General Arnaldo Ochoa.

Fidel's target was Ochoa, a discontented general and the most prestigious figure in the army. But he needed a reason to justify killing him and that reason was drug trafficking, which was Tony's field. Patricio had no involvement with drugs, but he could be useful to show how fair the Revolution was: kill the guilty twin but not the other who merely failed to correct his brother's excesses. That is why Patricio was allowed to live.

Fidel is a master of detail. He knew that the close friendship between Ochoa, Tony and Patricio would sooner or later turn them into the nucleus of an opposition that would be dangerous because of their combined experience and their appeal to the troops. Perilous times were on the horizon for Cuba that might lead to outbreaks of rebellion against the Maximum Leader if there existed a figure or group symbolizing that discontent. Perestroika was beginning to have an influence within the Ministry of the Interior, a stronger influence than most people imagined. Immediately after the Ochoa trial there was a complete dismantling of the Ministry of the Interior and a takeover by the armed forces. The ministry was suspect because it was a hub for people who had the most frequent contacts with foreign countries and with foreigners inside Cuba. They continued their task of training guerrillas, although aware that guerrilla warfare had no future in a world without the Soviet Union. They were also aware that in Latin America it was the process of democratization, not the process of revolution, that was irreversible.

I HAD TIME TO PREPARE MYSELF for the carrying out of the death penalty but not to prevent myself from being overwhelmed by the ironies. Tony could have been killed in Lebanon, in Chile, in Miami, or in any of the other places where he had carried out his secret missions. Ochoa might have died in battle in Angola, Venezuela, Nicaragua or Eritrea. That these men should meet with a violent death in Cuba was inconceivable. The Kafkaesque quality of the situation was intensified by our belief that since the triumph of the Revolution, no revolutionary had ever been executed, however serious the charges against him. Some had been sentenced to the ultimate penalty but they had always been pardoned. As it turned out, however, this too was one of the many lies Fidel had induced us to believe. Since the time of the Sierra Maestra, he had liquidated by execution every conceivable opponent.

After the tribunal's verdict, I still believed that the Council of State would exercise its right to grant a pardon. But when it gathered in an extraordinary session on July 9, the council unanimously ratified the verdict. Its members paraded in one by one, pronouncing themselves in favor of death—a macabre funeral march carried out by veterans of the Revolution, dignitaries of the regime and companions in arms of the condemned.

To conclude the session, Fidel turned his thumb down.

During the trial he had remained just offstage watching the sessions, hidden behind his two-way mirror. He later admitted meeting daily with the prosecutor, but "without trying to influence him," of course. It was like a B movie, scripted and directed entirely by Fidel.

Tony was allowed to receive one last visit from his family at the offices of military counterintelligence, near the airport. There were no illusions now about his fate. That same night, as a last resort, Ileana and I went to see the writer Gabriel García Márquez at the luxury residence in Siboney given him by Fidel. We arrived at one in the morning, almost running into Fidel, who, unknown to us, had just left. García Márquez was perhaps the only person capable of influencing Fidel, and moreover, he knew and esteemed the condemned men. (In Tony's ransacked house we had found a copy of García Márquez's book *The General in His Labyrinth,* which he had signed with the flattering dedication: "To Tony, who sows goodness.")

The writer let us in and offered us coffee. A picture that Tony had painted and presented to him was still hanging on the wall of his salon. García Márquez told us he had been very moved by the trial and that he was in disagreement with the death sentences. Ileana and I begged him to intervene. The Nobel Prize-winning author simply answered that he had just finished talking for a long time with Fidel, that neither friends nor enemies desired these executions and that we had to trust in the efficacy of discreet efforts being made on behalf of the condemned men.

The next day he left for Paris. We never saw him again.

We learned later that he had served in Europe as an unofficial ambassador for Fidel, in charge of explaining and justifying the executions.

There must have been hidden microphones in García Márquez's house. Either that or he reported on us, because next day I was called in to the Ministry of the Interior and they repeated to me the details of our conversation. Colomé Ibarra, the army general who had zebra skins I had brought him from Africa on his walls, had just been named interior minister, replacing Abrantes. He explained to me that the current state of public opinion did not permit the suspension of the executions. He added that I myself did not have anything to worry about; I could even continue working for intelligence. He added that I should try to make the family understand the rightness and necessity of the executions. I told him that I could not explain what I myself could not comprehend.

"With that attitude all you're doing is closing doors for yourself," he said.

When magic no longer works, terror remains. Fidel has always acknowledged his fascination with Robespierre. ("Cuba needs many Robespierres," he once said.) He has always been enchanted by the

Jacobin myth of a revolution besieged. This gives him the right repeatedly to "save" the Revolution by monopolizing power and searching for moral equilibrium by means of the guillotine's blade.

The Ochoa trial was presented as a necessity—an ethical necessity—in the struggle against corruption and privilege. The real message was that anyone who dares to think for himself loses his privileges, including the ultimate privilege of life itself.

AT FIVE IN THE MORNING OF JULY 13, I heard on the radio that they had carried out the sentence. The same day, Tony's wife received a simple card informing her that the body of her husband was buried in the Colón cemetery, in an unmarked grave, under the number 46,427.

A month after the firing squad, José Abrantes' turn came; there was another trial, behind closed doors this time. Against all the evidence, the trial was presented as having nothing to do with the previous one. Officially, the once powerful minister was tried and convicted for having lied about vital state information and for embezzlement. He was condemned and a short time later, according to the official version, he died of a heart attack. Abrantes was not yet fifty years old.

So goes the logic of Robespierre. One trial calls for the next, until no one is left other than the Great Helmsman himself—sole depositary of all legitimacy and all integrity, ultimate interpreter of the Revolution.

15
AFTERWORD

AFTER THE EXECUTIONS, I HAD but one goal: to get out of Cuba with Ileana. Life there was no longer bearable. Before our eyes the memory of Ochoa was gradually being erased from official history; his photo and reports of the actions he had led in Angola, previously always material for a government-sponsored legend, had disappeared from public view. As for Tony, his best paintings, which he had deposited prior to his arrest in the Fine Arts Foundation so that reproductions could be made for sale in Japan, were confiscated by state security. When we asked for them, we were told they had been lost. After stealing his life and his legend, they took from him his most intimate passion—his art.

I imagine that in most countries Ileana's desire to leave would have been readily understood and sympathized with. The government had killed her father and she had had nothing to do with the actions for which he had been tried, if such a travesty can be called a trial. However, when I requested permission to leave Cuba, the minister of the interior told me I was crazy.

"Don't you realize the danger for Cuba she would pose outside the country?" he demanded.

We were not allowed to leave. The persecution and harassments were incessant. In our fear we spoke with foreign journalists and human rights organizations. We had to keep constant track of each other, never daring to be apart even for an instant. The state had assigned a special security team to watch us, the whole de la Guardia family being subjected to ongoing, intrusive scrutiny. We had to learn to live knowing that we were being spied upon and followed, aware that our most personal conversations were being recorded and analyzed.

There were also manifestations of friendship. "Bolshevik" contin-ued to visit us, walking the ten kilometers to our house despite his crippled leg. My Salvadoran friends also showed solidarity. And I learned that Nelson Gutiérrez, the leader of the Chilean MIR, visited Cuba after the executions, and that when the Americas Department tried to justify them to him, he told them not to bother because in his view they had been political assassinations.

I was still officially on the payroll of the Ministry of the Interior, but I refused to cash my paychecks. One day in September 1990, the counterintelligence service required us to appear at the offices of the MC. The official in charge of our case greeted us—a certain Agustín—who without the slightest hesitation lectured me in front of Ileana that I was crazy to keep living with her, that my obstinacy had brought me nothing but trouble, and that if he were in my shoes, he would leave Cuba.

I told him that he reminded me of the Mexican proverb in which a prisoner tells the officer who is detaining him: "I am an honest man and they made you a lieutenant."

Things were just about to get out of hand when his superior offi-cer, a Colonel Salgado, burst into the office. He tried to calm us down and promised us a definitive answer to our demand for an exit visa. He kept his word. The next day he told us no.

"Ileana shall not leave Cuba. It's final. As for you, you can do what you want," he said.

At a loss for any other argument, I answered that he had forgot-ten one detail: I was an Argentine citizen, and according to Cuban law, since Ileana was married to an Argentine citizen she should be allowed to leave the country unless some charge was pending against her. (I had never imagined that one day I would feel obliged to resort to this.) If they did not let her leave or formally accuse her of some-thing, I would have no choice but to ask my embassy for protection.

Colonel Salgado threatened to expel me from Cuba and send me packing on the next plane to Argentina. I told him that to do so they would have to overpower me physically and put me in handcuffs and take me to the airport forcibly, and that he could remain assured this would cause a scandal abroad.

After this confrontation we began, under any pretext, to frequent the Argentine embassy. The team of spies could not know what we were doing inside, nor what I talked about with the diplomats. I told whoever would listen that I was in perfect health and that if I were suddenly to die of a heart attack, the authorities would be responsible.

I also began publicly to denounce the Cuban government at gatherings where foreign journalists were present. Knowing that there were concealed microphones, and indeed precisely for that reason, I invited over to my house the French journalist François Pisani—who of course couldn't get over his amazement—to give him some facts relating to the executions of Tony and Ochoa. The regime would have liked to retaliate, but I was, after all, "the son of Masetti."

After six weeks of this theater, the interior minister himself, General Colomé Ibarra, summoned Ileana. He stressed that he would prefer to see her alone because I had shown him disrespect.

To our great surprise, the minister told her that he was aware of her desire to leave and that everything was arranged for her departure: she could go directly to immigration to pick up the passports. The authorities had done their calculations. They had realized we would be more trouble in Havana than elsewhere, and sensed that I was willing to go much further in my denunciations of the regime. After more than a year of incessant struggle, we had managed to pry loose our exit permits.

They called us to the offices of the counterespionage service. They recommended that we demonstrate our gratitude to Fidel for the trust he had shown us by personally authorizing our departure: he was counting on us not to make any public statements and we were told to avoid journalists. We should know that the CIA would try to approach us and, in that eventuality, we should contact Cuban representatives. In conclusion, they reminded us that Ileana's uncle Patricio was still a prisoner.

"We're not threatening you," they said. "But any inopportune public statement could complicate his situation."

Euphoric at the idea of finally being able to make our getaway, we agreed to whatever they asked, thanked the commander in chief for his trust, and left.

The day before our departure, counterintelligence called us in again. It was an unreal scene. They had actually prepared a little farewell buffet.

This was in November 1990.

After the trial and the executions of Tony and Ochoa in July 1989, the Berlin Wall had fallen, Ceauşescu had been toppled in Romania, Czechoslovakia had experienced a political spring in wintertime, and the Sandinistas had lost the elections in Nicaragua.

WHEN WE LANDED IN MEXICO CITY, Ileana and I got off the plane and smiled at each other; at last we could feel at ease.

At that very instant, Pedro Catela appeared. He was an Argentine who had received military training in Cuba in the 1970s but was so inept that when he finished the courses he was exiled to Mexico and for years got along doing little favors for the Cuban government. But his luck eventually changed and he landed a job with the Mexican agency in charge of internal security. The agency's chief was Fernando Gutiérrez Barrios, a friend of Fidel Castro's since the time Castro had been in Mexico preparing his invasion of Cuba in the mid-1950s.

Catela approached us and made it clear he knew all about our situation. Emphasizing the fact that he was a Mexican official, he told us not to worry about anything, a statement which immediately made me start worrying. He said he could use his influence to get us residency and work permits. He suggested that we move into an apartment belonging to one of his friends until we could get permanently settled.

The message was clear: the Cuban government would continue keeping a close watch on us through its sympathizers in the Mexican security forces. I knew they would hold over my head my previous activities in Mexico City. And Ileana's situation was also precarious: she had only a one-month tourist visa.

From the moment we moved into the home of Catela's supposed friend, we knew that once again we were being watched, listened to, and spied upon. And Catela had kept our Mexican immigration forms. We would have to look for a way to escape.

We let three months go by. Our small supply of money was running out, and Catela was getting more and more oppressive; he even offered to set up a meeting for us with Cuba's intelligence station chief in Mexico City. Clearly the idea was that we needed to "get to work."

Acting as secretly as possible, we decided to buy ourselves exit visas. The problem was where to go. Which country would give a visa to Ileana with her damned Cuban passport?

A contact of ours in Cuba whose name I cannot reveal had told us before we left that a woman named Elizabeth Burgos had been in touch with him and that she had offered to help Tony's family any way she could. A Venezuelan who was once married to Régis Debray, the Frenchman who was imprisoned in Bolivia during the mid-1960s because he had joined Che's ill-fated guerrilla column in that Andean country, Burgos was living in Seville, Spain, where she worked as the director of the French Institute. The Cuban friend gave us her phone number.

In my paranoia, I hesitated before calling her. Who knew whether or not she too was working with the Cubans? But we had no other option. We finally risked calling her.

There was no need to give her any detailed explanations: Elizabeth had even fewer illusions about Cuba than we did. She was also well informed about the Cuban intelligence services. Her discretion and her tone—even on the telephone—but above all our need caused us to trust her. She said she would arrange a visa and put us up at her house.

Two days later Ileana's visa was waiting at the Spanish consulate. With the Spanish visa, and our exit permits—legal documents, albeit illicitly obtained—we left for Spain.

We weren't wrong about Elizabeth. Since then, she has been like family—our friend and our ally. The long arm of the Cuban Revolution still tries to touch us every now and then. But we have learned how to evade it.

IT WAS LEFT FOR ME TO DECIDE what to make of all this. As it happened, our year of forced residency in Cuba had not been a waste of time. It allowed me to undertake the task of reflection and arrangement of my thoughts, and to discover truths that out of a mixture of habit and vainglory I had previously refused to consider. The first thing, in fact, that became clear to me was that throughout my life there had been no shortage of wake-up calls that should have induced self-questioning, doubt and even indignation—but I had never picked up the phone.

In becoming a professional revolutionary, I, like so many others, had committed myself to a world in which there were only two sides— my side and the other side. Once committed to the logic of direct action, one avoids asking oneself about fundamental principles. One may feel confused at times, but the urgency of action always tends to suppress any nascent doubts. Obsessed by means, one forgets about ends. The urgency of action leaves no room to consider the big questions of good and evil. One simply forges ahead—first out of conviction, then out of inertia, stubborn in the championing of certain cast-iron postulates: for instance, that Cuba, seedbed of permanent revolution, was the most moral nation on earth.

During our internal exile in Cuba these muzzled questions finally began to bite. I found myself obsessed by a consuming need to review my life in an attempt to comprehend what had happened to me and why I had behaved as I had.

I tried to reach back and determine at what point I knew the Cuban Revolution had been betrayed. Obviously it was not in July 1989, but much earlier; I tried to fix the date. Perhaps the first intimation—after the death of Che—was when Castro supported and justified the intervention of Soviet armored forces in Czechoslovakia. Keeping a ruthless grip on power took priority, even at the cost of repressing a people who were in justified rebellion. But what Castro was defending was not, of course, the power solely of the U.S.S.R., but his own extravagant concept of personal power. The Soviets had done what he himself would do if his absolute command over Cuba were ever seriously challenged.

Yet there was no end to this process of reevaluation, no stopping point that would allow me to preserve the idea of a pure revolution betrayed—not 1968, not 1963, not 1961. As I thought about it—and once I had begun, I couldn't stop thinking about it—I had to admit that from its very origin, in the Sierra Maestra, the Revolution itself had been a fraud. Fidel Castro began by decapitating his own movement to seize absolute power for himself. No one would ever know how many of those who had participated in the struggle against Batista were shot after he was overthrown and Castro had taken power; how many died for the crime of demanding the democratic government promised them during the fight against the dictatorship. It is true that by 1961 most of the prison population on the island consisted of people who had fought against Batista. All of them were tried as Ochoa had been, with the same methods that had been applied since 1959: trumped-up charges of invented conspiracies. Thus was former rebel commander Sori Marín shot to death in 1961. Thus were ex-rebels Huber Matos and Mario Chanes de Armas (Fidel's comrade as far back as the ill-fated 1953 attack on Batista's army barracks at Moncada) condemned to twenty and thirty years' imprisonment respectively for the crime of preferring democracy over the dictatorship of the proletariat installed by the Maximum Leader.

Furthermore, I had to admit, as the American New Left of the 1960s had said, "the personal is the political." To see oneself as a future *comandante* is different from seeing oneself as an architect, a doctor or a family man. It was having a place in the history of our times, a possibility that Fidel Castro bestowed on us like a gift, that captivated young people, even though the truth was that he wanted to have history all to himself. I had joined the guerrillas as much because of

loneliness as because of conscience; because of my constant search
for a family; because of my need to belong to a group, to enter history and fulfill the destiny that had been imposed upon me by the
ghost of my father.

But what really was this history and destiny? With his infallible
political and strategic intuition, Fidel must have known that insert-
ing my father and the guerrilla column into the mountains of
Argentina was an operation destined to fail. There was not the remotest
chance that a guerrilla *foco* could be successfully established in the
Argentina of 1963. As I thought about it, I realized that my father had
been used to consolidate the myth of the Castroite guerrilla in the
continent. He was disposable, useful only as a symbol.

Fidel had known that Che, too, would fail in Bolivia. The position
of Che was based on a belief in vanguardism, that revolution was a
question of the will and the military capacity of an elite. But Che was
also manipulated, although he deserves part of the blame for what
happened in Cuba—and a substantial part. I say that he was manipulated because, even before he died, Fidel had already turned him
into the archetype of the "heroic guerrilla." Fidel knew that Che's
weak point was his sense that he was predestined to carry out a mission of salvation. I think that Che would have gone to Bolivia in any
case, but it is evident that Fidel hastened him on his way in order to
remove him from the scene. When Che left for Bolivia he had already
lost power in Cuba, but Fidel was very much aware of the fact that
Che, even though he might be wrong, thought for himself, and Fidel
foresaw that sooner or later the two men would come into conflict,
so he'd better get rid of Che. As he later did with Ochoa and so many
others.

Che and my father: I saw that I'd had a complicated relationship
with both of them. As "the son of Masetti," I was marked by my
father's legacy. From the time I was nine years old, they had put a
hero on my back and told me to become his equal. So coming to terms
with the Cuban Revolution and coming to terms with my father com-
prised a single act.

I decided that my relationship with my father has an intimate side,
which I keep to myself and regarding which I owe no explanations
to anyone. But there is also the relationship with the revolutionary
hero. Where that image is concerned, I have acquired a clearer idea
of what actually happened in the abortive campaign in which he died.
Becoming a sort of detective and taking this as my case, I discovered
that during his ill-fated and useless mission, my father had executed

three of his own men because of "weakness." Things went to that extreme because my father was someone with no military experience who suddenly found himself leading a guerrilla unit and instilling fear was the only way he could be sure his leadership was acknowledged. That's the method the Guevarista culture recommends: shoot the weak, those who express doubt.

My father was thirty-four when he himself was killed. I had expected that death would find me by the time I was thirty. I did everything I could to encounter my fate, but somehow it escaped me. During missions I sometimes felt the closeness of death, but detachedly, as though it were part of a game. But with the Ochoa trial I realized that if this was indeed what it was, it was yet a game played for keeps. To have died in Argentina, or in Nicaragua, or Angola or anywhere else the Revolution took me would have been the climax to my own chosen game. But then death made its appearance in Cuba and began to stalk our own people; to witness such a betrayal was to watch everything I believed in disintegrate.

Today I praise Tony and Patricio for their sensitivity, their artistic gifts. I praise my father for his benighted courage. But painful though it is for me to say, I cannot praise the mercenary roles that they—and I—played for Fidel Castro. I refuse to make heroes of men who, in some sense, were executioners. Yet I am aware that in other circumstances and with other possibilities before them, they might have become something other than what they were.

When I look at my life, and the lives of Tony and Patricio and so many others, I realize that the Revolution was a cover for committing atrocities without the slightest vestige of guilt. We told ourselves that we were doing good for humanity, when what really counted was single-minded purity of action.

We were young and irresponsible. We were pirates. We formed our own caste, separate even from revolutionaries who operated in their own countries and took up arms not as an esthetic choice, but as a response to local political circumstances. We belonged to and believed in nothing—no religion or flag, no morality or principle.

It's fortunate we didn't win, because if we had, we would have drowned the continent in barbarity. One of our slogans was to turn the Andes into the Sierra Maestra of Latin America: first we would have shot the military brass, then the oppositionists and then the *compañeros* who opposed our authoritarianism.

If the catastrophe of the trial and its tragic outcome had not intervened, I might have stayed in Cuba—both metaphorically and literally. To have acknowledged the barbarity of the Cuban Revolution would have unhinged me. I owe the life I have led since 1989 to Tony and his death, which liberated me.

Not long ago I visited Miami, where I met former Cuban political prisoners from the first years of the Revolution. I was surprised to find that they had fought against Batista, inspired by the same idealism that guided other young people of Latin America in their fights against the continent's dictatorships. But what surprised me most was the fact that they welcomed me into their midst in spite of the fact that I was a spoiled child of those who had imprisoned them.

This experience taught me that it is not enough to condemn Fidel Castro. You have to go further. It's easy to hide behind the excuse that you always acted honestly until you realized the truth. It's easy to say you were manipulated, just as it's easy to rationalize that despite all the abuses you committed, you were after all fighting against military dictatorships. You can't hold this part of your experience exempt from reevaluation. You have to shine a light on the dark side, the part of you that's attracted to power, the part that's drawn to cruelty, because we didn't try to destroy only our enemies, but we destroyed our women, our children, the people who worked with us. The fact is, during those years of conflict, all we did was destroy. We built nothing.

To ADMIT THE END OF AN ILLUSION and to move on in life has been my preoccupation over the last few years. I have undertaken this by putting together the pieces of myself that were left scattered about after the catastrophe of July 1989. Today, I can finally carry out the request that Tony made to me in that last letter which was handed to us the day after he was shot—a farewell letter written in pencil on a low-quality sheet of paper. There wasn't a single eraser mark. It was in the hasty handwriting of his final moments, hurried by his impatient guards.

Two letters on the same sheet. The letter on the front side was for me:

> Dear Jorge,
>   As I wrote to Ili, for me you are a son, not a son-in-law. First, because you're the son of a martyr of the revolution whom I greatly admired, and, second, because of your qualities as an internationalist revolutionary, selflessness and sincerity. I recognize in you the personal valor that you have demonstrated on many occasions from

an early age. I hope you'll give a fraternal embrace to Alejandro, who, although he may not know it, I always remembered as a brave and sincere person since the time we were in Nicaragua.

Jorge, I'm very grateful for the support that you've given to my family, especially to Ili and to my children and to Mary. Take care of my parents. They love you very much. I also ask that you start writing the book about your father, that would mean so much for Cuba. If only we could have kept working together many years. I know that you would have helped me very much. Urge Ili to begin working as soon as possible. That would help her a lot. Take care of her. She loves you very much. Give a big kiss to Conchita and tell her that I love her like a sister and that I beg her forgiveness. Explain everything to her. I needn't tell you that you are more revolutionary than ever because that is in your blood.

A big hug from your father,
Tony

On the back were his last words for Ileana:

My Dear Precious Ili,

I have no more time. I can only tell you again how much I have loved you and how much you mean to me, what you have taught me and shown me at the end of life about yourself—a truly human being, my love. Your character has impressed me, I didn't know you, this has fortified me more than you could imagine, as it has Mary. You have set an incomparable example. I can't believe that there are many revolutionaries like you. I hope I had some influence on your development. My love, love Jorge very much. Remember to help Mimi and Popín, Mary and all your brothers and sisters. I tell you again today that there are very few women like you and I feel very proud. I know that you are going to be an example for us all. I have no words to describe my love for you. I only ask that you always live proud of your father, and of your brothers and sisters. Help them. I love you with all my soul and again I love you.

Your father,
Tony

Written moments before he was marched to the firing squad, Tony's words reveal him trying to find dignity in his status as a revolutionary to the very end. Like this entire story, like the trial, like the confessions, his words are part of a sad enigma.

But this much is clear: Tony asked me to write a book about my father, a book that would mean much for Cuba, that would define what it was and what it is. He probably envisioned a book about the principles of the Cuban Revolution, of the enthusiasm of its first moments, of the era of Che and a generous internationalism. But in his letter, Tony also says that he adopts me as a son and he signs as a father. So may he grant a father's forgiveness if what I have written is not quite what he might have wanted, but is nonetheless the truth about his life and mine.

INDEX